On Leatherwood Creek

Dutchtown boys grew up in poverty and fought W W II as teenagers to take their place in the Greatest Generation

T/Sgt. James Lee Hutchinson
Celebrating Indiana's Bicentennial

authorHOUSE®

AuthorHouse™
1663 Liberty Drive
Bloomington, IN 47403
www.authorhouse.com
Phone: 1 (800) 839-8640

Published by AuthorHouse   10/13/2016

ISBN: 978-1-5246-4308-9 (sc)
ISBN: 978-1-5246-4307-2 (e)

Library of Congress Control Number: 2016916425

Print information available on the last page.

Author s Honors

It was my privilege to have the State of Indiana honor Lee Hutchinson by Special Resolution, which not only honored his valuable service to the United States during World War II, but also honored him as a unique Hoosier author.

Through his down-home insight about life in Indiana, interspersed with his candor and sense of humor, Lee has done something I have always wanted to do – write a book about how our generation grew up. The things he did as a child will be of great interest to generations to follow in this electronic age.

Respectfully, Brent Steele Indiana State Senator

State of Indiana

Indiana General Assembly

SENATE CONCURRENT RESOLUTION FIFTY

A CONCURRENT RESOLUTION Honoring World War II Veteran James Lee Hutchinson of Bedford, Indiana.

Whereas, Between 1944 and 1945, James Lee Hutchinson served with the "Mighty Eighth" Air Force - the most decorated U.S. Army Air Corps Unit during WWII;

Whereas, James served as a radio operator and gunner on a lead crew of the B-17 Flying Fortress during eighteen combat missions with the 490th Bomb Group of the 8th Air Force in England;

Whereas, James and his nine fellow crew members joined hundreds of other bombers as they went on numerous missions into the heart of Hitler's Germany. They flew at 25,000 feet, on oxygen, in sub-zero temperatures for hours at a time facing anti-aircraft flak and attacks by Luftwaffe fighters;

Whereas, Upon returning from the war at age 20, James attended Indiana University where he majored in

Mayor Shawna Girgis and Governor Mike Pence honored me as Grand Marshall of the 2015 Bedford Heritage Festival Parade.

Thanks to Governor Pence for the Keynote address, Indiana Medallion and riding with me in the 2015 July 4th Bedford Limestone Heritage Parade

CITY OF BEDFORD

Proclamation

TO ALL WHOM THESE PRESENTS MAY COME, GREETINGS:

WHEREAS: The City of Bedford, and its citizens are here to give thanks and to show our appreciation to James Lee Hutchinson for his outstanding citizenship, dedication, and leadership he has shown throughout our community and our country, and

WHEREAS: Lee and his late wife June had been married 67 years. They have two daughters: Sherri Alexander, and Susan Hutchinson; five granddaughters: Mary Ann Muckerheide, Laura Alysworth, Lisa Dahl, Shannon Irmscher, and Stacy Musunuru; nine great-grandsons; and one great-granddaughter; and

WHEREAS: Lee was just out of high school when he first saw the B-17, he was drafted at the age of 18 upon his high school graduation. He served as a radio operator/gunner on the Lt. William D. Templeton crew of the 490th Bomb Group H, Squadron 848 at Eye, England; and

WHEREAS: Lee entered Indiana University on the G.I. Bill and earned three degrees. He was an elementary school teacher, principal and assistant superintendent for 37 years, he retired in 1987; and

WHEREAS: Lee loves his role as a storyteller and educating this generation. He has completed four books of not only his stories but also stories of other WWII veterans. Lee has recorded and preserved more than 500 veterans' stories as well as his own. He was honored in the United States Congress on February 18, 2008, by Joint Resolution 50 and was also honored in the Indiana General Assembly for his work in preserving the history of the Greatest Generation; now

THEREFORE: I Shawna M. Girgis, Mayor of the City of Bedford, Indiana, do hereby proclaim Saturday, July 4th, 2015 as

"JAMES LEE HUTCHINSON DAY"

In Bedford and urge all citizens to join me in thanking him for his leadership, dedication, and inspiration. May we never forget the men and women who have fought for our country and our freedom.

IN WITNESS THEREOF, I hereunto have set my hand and caused to be affixed the Great Seal of the City of Bedford, Indiana, on this 4th day of July, 2015.

Shawna M. Girgis
Mayor of Bedford

"In 2008, I was pleased to honor James Lee Hutchinson on the Floor of the Indiana House of Representatives upon the publication of his first book, "Through These Eyes". His fifth book "On Leatherwood Creek" represents his latest contribution to the preservation of history for future generations."

Indiana State Representative Eric Koch

Indiana Lt. Governor Becky Skillman received a copy of "Through These Eyes A World War II Eighth Air Force Combat Diary" from the author James Lee Hutchinson at the 2007 Bloomington Memorial Day ceremony.

Congressman Todd Young of Indiana's Ninth Congressional District presents a Congressional Veterans Commendation which was read into the Congressional Record December 8, 2015.

Congressional Record

United States of America

PROCEEDINGS AND DEBATES OF THE 114th CONGRESS, FIRST SESSION

| Vol. 161 | WASHINGTON, TUESDAY, DECEMBER 8, 2015 | No. 177 |

HONORING JAMES "LEE" HUTCHINSON

HON. TODD C. YOUNG
OF INDIANA
IN THE HOUSE OF REPRESENTATIVES
Tuesday, December 8, 2015

Today, we honor James "Lee" Hutchinson for his service to his country and to his community. A southern Indiana native, Hutchinson served with the US Army Air Corps during the final years of World War II. After attending training to become a radio operator, Hutchinson shipped out with the 490th Bombardment Group of the 8th Air Force. While serving with the "Mighty Eighth," Hutchinson was aboard a B-17 Flying Fortress; he and his crew executed missions deep within Nazi Germany, and often faced anti-aircraft fire and attacks by the German Luftwaffe.

Hutchinson's numerous awards and commendations include, among others, a World War II Victory Medal, European African Middle Eastern Service Medal, and an American Theater Service Medal.

He arrived home at the age of 20 and enrolled in Indiana University with a desire to study history and journalism. He pursued further education after graduating with a Bachelor of Science degree in Education in 1949, and enjoyed a 37 year career in education in the Bedford-North Lawrence school system. Hutchinson's experiences in World War II inspired him to author "Through These Eyes: A World War II Eighth Air Force Combat Diary," which chronicled his life in the US Army Air Corps. Hutchinson published three more books that detail memorable moments from his life and highlight his record of service.

An accomplished author, educator, and serviceman, Hutchinson remains involved in his home church. Moreover, he served as the president of the local Rotary Club, and is an active member of his Masonic Lodge.

Dedicated to

The memory of my wonderful wife, family, friends and co-workers who enriched my life and supported me in my long march out of the Depression into a wonderful life in the Greatest Generation!

Contents

Introduction

Time is a gift from God, spend it wisely
It has an expiration date!

The Thomas Wolfe novel, <u>You Can't Go Home Again</u>, 1940 stated you can't recover the past. That may be true but at the age of ninety-one I can share my memories with this generation. The short stories in this book tell some of the history of my boyhood, family and friends who enriched my life in the Great Depression. It is a 'pre-quel' to my first four books to tell of happy times and hardships which provided children of my generation the grit and determination to survive and win World War II.

The names of my boyhood pals are a composite of many buddies of my childhood and I have used the short story format and sixth grade vocabulary to encourage reading for ages twelve to ninety. My sketches and photos help set the scene and each short story stands alone but are more or less in order of events and seasons. They also signify that I qualify as a starving artist.

Our lives were not complicated by bathrooms, air conditioning, television, computer games or cell phones. We were out in the fresh air, organized our own games and free to roam the streets, fields or woodlands of the neighborhood. We had strict discipline in school, chores at home and every family member contributed to the family operation. Most families were striving to survive and rear their children to be law abiding citizens. Mothers stayed home to cook and take of the children while fathers worked to support the family. There were many homes without electricity or water and few houses had telephones or central heat. Those conditions were not unusual for the time, rather they were the norm. The majority of Southern Indiana families were in the same economic situation as mine in to the Great Depression prior to World War II.

I have witnessed the growth and change of the USA from radio days to television, computers, cell phones and drone bombers. It has been an amazing journey through time and history. The changes in society and government according to our Constitution, religion, education and science are amazing. I thank God I have been privileged to tell my story in four books and record those of many other World War ll veterans slowly fading into history. We were young and sixteen million strong when we served on land sea and air around the world to defeat three powerful military forces determined to conquer the our country. The cost was high, thousands died and millions were wounded. Most have passed, but their heroic flights are saved in four books. I report WW II history as a man who was there as a teenager. I do not consider the task finished and continue to speak and write as a 'Living Antique' to tell stories of the Greatest Generation and honor fellow WW II veterans.

My boyhood experiences in Southern Indiana during in the Great Depression were much the same as many World War II veterans. The Depression was more than a decade of poverty and hardship and there is a great need to tell this generation of the patriotism and sacrifices made in protecting our nation.

"We enjoyed our freedom, never dreaming that as teenagers, we would be sent halfway around the world to protect it with our lives'.

Chapter 1

Roots

Dad grew up on a large farm in Southern Indiana. He was the oldest of eight children and shared the many farm chores with five brothers and two sisters. He quit school at sixteen to help his parents on the farm. Like most tillers of the soil, Grandpa Isaac Newton Hutchinson and Grandma Della Mae needed a large family to eke out a living on their 180 acres. Grandpa Newt and the older boys tilled the land with teams of horses or mules, fattened the pigs and milked a herd of cows to feed the family while Grandma and younger kids tended to the chickens, gardening and canning. Family food and income came from the farm animals and crops were produced from long days of hard labor. They exemplified the old proverb:

Edmund Terrell - It is amazing that history can reveal a great deal about your ancestors. I recently discovered a story to share with my family. Indiana declared statehood in 1816 and the Hutchinson family settled in the Leesville area shortly afterwards. Pioneer Edmund Terrell was killed and scalped by a band Indians while working in a clearing near his cabin in 1820. The Indians also attacked Terrell's log cabin. His wife escaped but they took his twelve year old daughter Sally captive and planned to take her to their village in Northern Indiana. Sally managed to escape after a few days on the trail and find her way back to Leesville. Terrell also had a son Robert and his daughter, Margaret later married Charles Hutchinson. One of their sons was Joseph Hutchinson, who

1

married Elizabeth Mc Cleery and they were the parents of Issac Newton Hutchinson, my Grandpa.

"A farmer works from sun to sun; a farm wife's work is never done." Children were assigned chores according to their ages and in those days (1914) it was common for the oldest son to drop out of school to work on the farm. Dad finished the eighth grade at Leesville School before joining the family business. It was generally agreed that you didn't need a high school diploma to milk cows, walk behind a plow or harvest crops.

Mother was also an Indiana farm girl, but Granddad Claude James Hoar was never a landowner. He was a proud man who could trace his ancestors back to a graveyard in England. Bad luck made him a tenant farmer with a wife and three children to support. He was forced to move many times because jobs, seasonal work and housing determined where the family would live. Tractors and trucks were rare in farming and large farm owners employed several farm-hands to work with the horse-drawn equipment. Aunt Em's farm in the Wizard of Oz was an example of self-sufficient farmers who hired several farmhands to help plant, plow and harvest crops. Grandmother Fannie Hoar died of the 'milk sickness' and childbirth at age twenty-nine. My mother was five years old and her brothers were three and seven when their mother died. Granddad attempted to carry on with three children under the age of ten. He then married a widow with older children, but that marriage failed. Grandmother's relatives helped care for mother and her brothers while Granddad worked on nearby farms and the children attended various one room country schools. I have one school photo of Mom at age fourteen at the Martinsburg school near Pekin, Indiana. Little brother Ralph was also in the picture. Older brother, Bruce was enrolled in Pekin High School and later graduated. Mother dropped out at age sixteen to keep house for her Dad while her brothers completed their education. Farm jobs became scarce on small Indiana for greener pastures. The flat prairies of Illinois had better and richer farming areas and it was easy to find work and many families decided to leave the hill farms of Southern Indiana for more fertile fields.

Mother's large family of six uncles, the Marshalls sold out, packed their to move to central Illinois. Granddad decided to join his in-laws and said goodbye to his brothers Clark and Charlie. The family clan settled in Illinois areas around Mattoon and Lincoln where there were plenty of farm jobs for men to labor with horse drawn equipment. A few years later my Dad, Clyde Ernest Hutchinson of Leesville, Indiana joined a traveling wheat threshing crew which followed the harvest across Indiana to work on large Illinois farms. Near the town of Lincoln, he met and married Essie Elizabeth Hoar an eighteen year old girl who missed the hills of Southern Indiana. The newlyweds returned to Indiana to set up housekeeping in a four room board and batten tenant house across the valley from the big red brick house on his Uncle Emory's farm.

On June 12, 1925, Dr. Woolery of Heltonville, Indiana made a house call at the tenant house and that was the day I became a Hoosier. My first dog, Collie, was there waiting for me. I seems as though I have dogs all my life. The following Spring I had pneumonia and old Doc Woolery said I might live or die. However, my parents decided to make a visit to Illinois in their new Model T Ford, I guess they wanted Mom's family to see the baby before he died!

I was three when Dad decided to quit farming and go to work in a Bedford, Indiana limestone mill. His brothers helped build a new house of native lumber on Grandpa Hutchinson's farm. The small house faced the county road leading from Highway 50 into Leesville. They carried household water from a hillside spring near the creek running through the valley behind the house. One hot August day a flock of relatives came to our house when we weren't expecting company and an aunt took my hand to lead me down over the hill to get a bucket of water. She let me play in the cool creek water a long time that hot afternoon and when we climbed the hill back to the house and I heard a baby crying. Dr. Woolery had made another house call and baby sister Jean had arrived. I was no longer an only child and I decided I wasn't going back to the spring again!

Later, Dad sold the house and we moved to a tenant house on the Rariden Hilltop Dairy farm on Bedford's outskirts to be closer to his job in the stone mill. He fed and tended a herd of young cows in return for free rent. Our driveway was a few hundred feet from a pleasant creek called Leatherwood. We crossed an 1896 arched bridge over the creek in our Model A and climbed Slaughterhouse Hill to get into town. Things were going fairly well for Dad, so he bought a run-down four room fix-up house on a large lot in the southeast edge of Bedford. Unfortunately, the deal was completed shortly before the stock market crashed. The little house had no utilities, we carried water from a neighbor, used kerosene lamps, and heated with wood or coal stoves. A few months later, my baby brother, Kenny joined the family and the five of us settled down just in time for the deepest part of the 'Great Depression.'

Depression Bedford

Our little house was in the southeast corner of Bedford, Indiana in a neighborhood called Dutchtown due to the large number of German families having homes in that section of town. We had a brick German-American Church with a tall steeple and a bell we could hear many blocks away. Italian and many other nationalities had settled in the area to work in the stone industry and their talents ranged from stone carvers to laborers in the quarries. Our monumental stone Catholic Church with even louder bells was a block farther west. Every dog in Dutchtown howled when the bells began clanging and all sinners knew it was Sunday morning.

Our pleasant neighborhood was a little like Andy Griffth's Mayberry, with relatives, friends and town characters who were a very important part of my life in the poverty of the Great Depression. It was a neighborhood where everyone knew everybody's business, their problems and triumphs. The information was not only in the form of gossip, but care and concern for others. Windows were open all summer, closed only by a hard rain, and a good family argument could provide entertainment for the entire neighborhood! Few people had phones and those who did were hooked to a 'party line' to share with four or more neighbors. Customers could (and often did) listen in on much of the conversation. Gossip was a lot harder to gather during winter months, but the eavesdroppers generously shared with their neighbors. Keeping secrets was a tough job and the local gossips considered the 'party line' a wonderful invention!

Bedford was the Lawrence County seat with a large limestone courthouse in the middle of the square which was the center-piece of town. Buildings around the town square were independently owned shops and stores along with a few chin stores like SS Kressge, Woolworth, Montgomery Ward and J.C. Penney. Saturday was 'trading day' when every store was open until 9:00 p.m. and county people came to town to shop and visit. Parking spaces were at a premium as families would park, roll down the windows and stay for hours to watch the pedestrians on parade. Many families brought picnic baskets to avoid the two bits cost of the 'blue plate' meals in restaurants. Others dined on ten cent sandwiche. Our three movie theaters operated five nights a week. On weekends, it was two movies and a serial from noon until 11:00 p. m. plus the Saturday Midnight Show!

Our little town had a population of 12,000, was an active community. The small shops and family owned business around the courthouse square had not yet faced the giant superstores of today. Today, we old-timers meet for morning coffee and talk about days when money was scarce and the town square was our business and shopping center. Our local museum has a mural of the stores around the square before supermarkets and retail giants closed the family-owned groceries and most small specialty stores. Today, most are gone and chain stores have moved to the four-lane highway by-pass. Semi-trucks haul the merchandise and Railroads have faded into history.

The Monon Railroad ran north and south smack dab through the town square and the Milwaukee rails ran east and west just two blocks north. Streets were blocked and traffic halted two or three time daily while long trains snaked their way through town.

Black smoke rolled from the coal-fired steam locomotives but there were few complaints, trains were important to our economy. Bedford sits in the middle of a geographical area containing large limestone deposits formed in prehistoric ages. City and Lawrence County officials cherished the title of 'Limestone Capital of the World' and railroads hauled the heavy stone to building sites across the nation.

Stone quarries dotted the countryside as various companies searched and explored for lodes of high quality limestone. Hundreds of men labored to dig giant blocks of the grey stone from the hills to be hauled to stone mills to be cut, carved and prepared for construction of famous state and federal buildings. Stonecutters, carvers and sculptors came from Europe to profit from their talents. Skilled architects and draftsmen designed beautiful buildings and skilled artisans produced excellent work from statues to giant scrolls to add to a building's beauty. The Empire State Building, National Cathedral, state capitols and federal buildings in Washington D. C. provide examples of Indiana limestone. Stone quarries of huge holes in Southern Indiana and modern stone mills produce the durable limestone today.

The limestone industry provided many jobs for the area. Approximately 4,600 men were working in the twelve quarries and twenty-five mills in the area in 1923, and 30,000 flat-bed rail cars of stone were shipped to building projects. Hourly wages in 1928 were: stonecutters $1.25, stone planners 90 cents and laborers at 45 cents. Hundreds of workers labored to quarry out top quality Indiana limestone to be used across the United States for state, federal and commercial buildings still in use. Limestone is one of the most durable building materials and there were more than twenty quarries and/or stone mills operating in Lawrence County before the Great Depression squelched the demand. The empty quarries and stone mills across Indiana stood idle until the building boom that came after World War II.

Lawrence County was caught in the midst of the world-wide Depression which followed the First World War. Many of the skilled artisans left for greener pastures, but local laborers who had purchased homes in the area had no choice but to stay and sweat out the depression. Dad was one of those guys who had a good job in a stone mill and planned to move up in the world, but hard times came to southern Indiana shortly after he moved our family to town. The national employment hovered around twenty five percent in late 1929, but it was a much higher percentage in our county because we were a one industry town and that industry had been shut down. Our nation was in a Depression and the demand for durable building material ended, so Southern Indiana limestone quarries and mills stood idle. Few realized the high national unemployment rates would last until 1942 and the beginning of WW II. Our family was one of many who lost their homes. However, the bank had too many empty houses and rented back to Dad for five dollars a month!

Jobs were as scarce as hen's teeth and consisted mostly of short term chores for farmers or local businesses. Men were willing to work for a dollar a day and neighbors traded labor or services with no money involved. Deals like, 'You help me spade my garden and I'll help you patch your roof' were sensible ways to make-do without money. The honor system worked and people paid back what they had borrowed in one form or the other. It was a time when help or labor was something you could give your neighbor and he was there you when you needed a helping hand. Poor people were all in the same boat and a most deals were settled with a promise or handshake. A common adage was, "A man is only as good as his word." Trading labor or lending possessions was used on a regular basis and the payment was usually,

"Thanks a heap, I'm obliged to ya' and I'll pay you back some day."

Borrowing a cup of sugar or trading garden products was common among women in the neighborhood. Most families planted gardens and had a small henhouse on the alley. Gardens provided fresh vegetables to be sold or canned. Chickens in backyard coops produced eggs for food or sale and old hens who didn't produce became special guests at Sunday dinners. Crowing roosters at sunrise served as neighborhood alarm clocks and were accepted as a necessary nuisance.

House at 2426 H Street

Our little four room board and batten house was located at the south end of the fine concrete slab that was H Street, but alas, water and sewer lines had never been installed on our side of the street. Our outhouse was a two-holer nailed to the garage down on the alley. Today, a realtor would list it as 'four rooms and a path'. Ou lot was three feet below street level and the city had installed an iron rail on the sidewalk to keep people from falling off the sidewalk into our front yard. Neighborhood kids used it as a Jungle Gym.

That unpainted four room rectangle of about a thousand square feet with no water, electricity or central heat and a tar paper roof that leaked like a sieve provided a home for two adults and three kids for six years. Dozens of pots and buckets were needed to catch the leaking water during rainstorms. Dad mopped the roof with melted tar each summer, but he fought a losing battle. My parents made an arrangement with our new neighbor, Auggy, to pay part of his water bill so they could carry buckets of water from a faucet in his basement. This was a perfect example of how people helped each other in those desperate days of the Depression when everybody needed help in one form or another. We needed water and Auggy needed good company. He was a veteran of the First World War who lived alone and was really glad to have our family as his new neighbors. Auggy didn't talk much about his thirteen years in the army, but through the years I heard a few tales of his military experiences. He became a longtime family friend, almost an uncle to three towhead kids as we grew into adults. However, at that time, he had a second reason to give a warm welcome to our family. His former neighbors were two business women of the 'oldest profession' who had far too many late night 'customers.' Mom and Dad discovered that fact soon after moving into the house. Several nights during the first weeks, men would stand out on the sidewalk and yell to ask if they were open for business. The 'callers' got their answer when Dad charged out on the porch waving his shotgun to give them a 'cussin' and tell 'em the 'goodtime girls' had moved to a new location down the block!

The Kitchen

The kitchen was the heart of my early childhood home. A long counter with a dry sink, table, chairs and huge wood- burning cook-stove filled the room. Our kitchen table was a multiple-use piece of furniture. The big round oak table served as an eating surface, ironing board, space for preparing food and a game board. We often used it for table-top games with marbles, cards and coloring books. It became a desk in the evening, as we sat around it to do our homework. We had no electricity and we studied by the light of a kerosene (coal oil) lamp. When the sun sank slowly in the west, it was time to remove the glass globe, strike a match and light a lamp wick dipping down into kerosene. The yellow-orange flame didn't give much light, but you could turn up the flame to read, play games or do homework when it was sitting in the middle of the round kitchen table.

The lamp's wicks had to be trimmed often or they would smoke like a freight train and blacken the fragile glass globes Lamps were dangerous, but much better than candles. Moving from room to room at night meant taking a lamp to light the way. They were portable but hot and you needed to carry it gently and keep it level. The flame on the braided cloth wick and the kerosene were separated by an inch or less and there was always the danger of dropping the hot lamp and starting a fire. The chores of trimming wicks, washing globes and re-filling them disappeared when we moved to a house with electricity. Coal oil kitchen stoves were used in some homes, but Mom cooked on a wood fired kitchen stove.

Cold and rainy days would find us enjoying the warmth of the big black cook-stove. The stove was so old that the metal on the side of the firebox had burned out and we could sit by the side of the stove and enjoy the heat of the cherry flames nibbling at the oak wood. It was like having a fireplace in the kitchen. The flames and the steaming teakettle filled the room with warmth and humidity. We had a Depression humidifier and enjoyed it. Dad liked oak firewood because it split into small sticks easily and gave off a lot of heat. He used it or hickory in the living room stove when coal wasn't available.

The kitchen stove top had four removable lids on the cooking surface which could be lifted with a special handle. Mom used a short poker to re-arrange the burning coals or shove more firewood into the firebox through a door on the front. There was a cavernous oven for baking, a reservoir (water tank) on the side for warming water. Mom liked to keep it full, because the only other water in the house w as the tea kettle and water bucket.

The hot black stovepipe which carried smoke to the brick chimney in the wall behind the stove passed through a long warming oven compartment above the cooking surface. Stovepipes were also a fire hazard, the thin metal could burn through and fill the house with smoke. A creosote fire in the chimney flue could also burn down a house and Bedford fire trucks were busy during cold weather. One daily chore was keeping the wood box behind the stove full of dry wood and kindling, but I also kept an eye on that stovepipe. I remember the day Dad bought Mom a new green and cream-colored Kalamazoo cook-stove for thirty-six dollars. The old stove went to the junkyard and we were happy to wave goodbye to the burned-out firebox before it burned our little house down. (Two generations later, two of our granddaughters graduated from Western Michigan University in Kalamazoo.) Now, if we wanted to watch dancing flames, we went into the living room to the pot-bellied Warm Morning stove and see flames through the glass windows in the door. The cook-stove was one of our most versatile pieces of equipment. Cooking and baking was our first priority, but it was also used to heat water on bath and wash days, heating sad irons on ironing day. Leftovers were usually a pot of beans on the back of the stove and biscuits or cornbread in the warming oven. Some days Mom would whip up a large pot of soup from a soup bone or small piece of beef and rice to last several meals. Potato soup was also on the menu quite often because 'taters were easy to store and save long after the gardens were covered with snow.

Mom was a good cook and skillfully used anything available. She could prepare a good meal with anything from fish, squirrel or rabbit to government surplus. Of course we were always hungry and easy to please. I remember Dad soppin' up gravy with a biscuit to get every bit of food in his plate and Mom teased him about not having to wash his plate. I also became an expert 'sopper' and cleaned my plate at every meal. We didn't need a garbage can and Collie only got a scrap from the table when Mom and Dad were looking the other way. There were no neatly packed cartons of 'instant' meals or frozen foods. She spent many hours cooking from scratch and was often up to her elbows in flour when making dough and rolling it out for dumplings or pie crust. Biscuits called for flour, cornbread called for cornmeal and Mom baked according to the available supplies. She cooked large meals and made a warmed-over meal taste just as good or better than the first time. Our breakfast menu varied from oatmeal, biscuits and gravy, flap Jacks to bacon and eggs. In the early winter, when it got cold enough for Grandpa to butcher a hog, we had fresh meat for a few days. Lard was used in all food preparation and fried potatoes were my favorite, second only to fried sweet potatoes. Chicken and dumplings made any Sunday special. Cheap cuts of pork boiled with rice, potatoes or cabbage was also well received and sausage gravy was a real treat. Beans were always a basic meal with cornbread or biscuits and she often put dumplings in the beans

Cooking meals was a problem in the summer. Mom would fire up the kitchen stove early in the morning. Breakfast didn't take a lot of heat, but cooking dinner and supper from scratch was another matter. The house stayed hot all day when she baked cornbread or cooked up a pot of beans. The trees in the backyard were a blessing and we enjoyed many summer days out in their shade to escape the stifling heat. Dad would build a fire in a stone fire-pit in the backyard to avoid building up heat in the house and Mom often had a pot of soup or beans cooking in the backyard. We had lot of picnic meals during the 'dog days' of summer and we dined well on peanut butter and jelly, buttered crackers or butter or sugar sandwiches.

Wash Day

Monday was washday which meant a long hard day's work carrying buckets of water to heat on the stove. Dad used the backyard fire-pit to heat enough water to fill two ten gallon galvanized wash tubs on hot summer washdays. The clothes needed to be soaked in a tub of hot soapy water, scrubbed on a washboard with a big bar of yellow OK soap and rinsed in a second tub. Mom would wring clothes by hand before lugging a basket out to a clothesline to hang them in the in the sunshine. She earned a long rest in the shade and several glasses of cool water from the icebox on Mondays.

Every house had a clothesline of two or three wire or rope lines mounted on posts, stretched across the backyard. Every piece of clothing was hung on the line with wood clothes- pins to wave recklessly in the breeze and be dried by the sun. There were early spring or fall days when the wet washing froze before it dried. Rain or winter weather forced housewives to dry clothing indoors on wooden racks, furniture or makeshift lines. Winter washdays were exciting because Mom put up temporary clotheslines in the two heated rooms and we romped and played in a maze of hanging sheets, towels and clothing dangling from makeshift clotheslines. Eventually, she made a deal to use Auggy's washing machine in his basement in return for doing his laundry. That electric washer with the roller wringers made washday a whole lot easier and was a great improvement in both in time and labor. Baths were taken in the same tubs in the kitchen behind the warm stove. We used a sheet hanging on a rope line for privacy.

Tuesday was ironing day was and the sad irons were heated on the kitchen stove. Handles on the old one-piece irons got so hot they had to be wrapped in a cloth. Newer models had removable wood handles so she could keep one heating on the stove to replace one when it cooled. She set up an ironing pad on the kitchen table, sprinkled the piece to be ironed and ironed away. We didn't have a lot of clothing, but we went to school in clean duds.

Wednesdays and Thursdays were baking days when she baked our family's weekly supply of yeast buns and naturally, every hungry kid in the neighborhood wanted to play at our house on days when she brought those tasty buns out of the oven and let us share with hungry buddies. They were delicious when steaming hot and smeared with butter and mustard! She baked several pans on early summer mornings in order to let the house cool down. That wasn't a problem on winter days because the stove was needed to back for the big coal stove in the front room heat the house. She baked several pans, wrapped them in cotton towels and stored them in a mouse-proof five gallon tin lard can. Mom's yeast buns where a treat, like white bread from the grocery store and a welcome change from soda biscuits. The supply was supposed to last a week, but it usually came up a few days short. Friday she cleaned house, wrapped up all the loose ends and hoped for restful weekend.

The water bucket was a very important piece of equipment for families without plumbing, especially when you were thirsty. It was usually the only water in the house if Mom needed some for cooking. She kept a small washpan in the dry sink for washing hands. We carried city water from a faucet in Auggy's basement for drinking, cooking and laundry. Several neighbors had concrete cisterns buried in their backyard to collect rainwater from their roofs for washing. Our water was much better because it came from Auggie's basement. Mom kept our water bucket in the coolest and darkest corner of the kitchen dry sink counter where the sun never shone. She draped a clean linen cloth over it to keep out thirsty flies and other winged insects. A battered aluminum dipper lay on the counter beside it, but thirsty little kids had trouble managing a drink from a long-handled dipper and yelled for help when they were dry. It was always wise to check for unwanted items like bugs, when you drank warm water from the bucket. Water from the town pump on the way to school was much cooler. Summer drinks were much better when we got an ice-box and could keep a Mason jar full on ice. We enjoyed free cold drinks in the winter and some mornings when the kitchen stove had burned low during the night, we had to break the ice and move the water bucket much closer to the stove.

Mom used to say the only time we our house had running water was during a heavy rain when the roof leaked! One joker said he had running water because he had to run to the well to get it. Our water bucket might do double-duty and join all the pots and pans placed around in the house to catch water when we had a thunderstorm. I remember Mom and Dad taking turns emptying buckets or pots during a heavy storm. On warm dry summer days, neighborhood men often brought out their ladders and traded labor to seal or patch neighborhood roofs with hot tar.

Living Room

Our living room and family room was a ten by twelve foot room in the front of the house. The front door led to the porch. Lighting for the entire room came from a coal-oil lamp sitting on a stand-table between Mom and Dad's rocking chairs. The little table they sat around over eighty years ago now sits in the living room of my youngest daughter.

The living room was the center of family activity on evenings when we needed a fire in the pot-bellied coal stove. Heat drifted in from the kitchen, but the big Warm Morning stove was our major source of warmth and furnace in extremely cold weather. It sat unused in fair weather but there were many winter nights when it was roaring hot and rosy red. Some nights the stove pipe would get too hot and there was always the threat of a flue fire with fire and sparks blowing out the chimney. There were house fires each winter and the Fire Department had a lot of business during cold weather.

We dragged in a kitchen chair or played on the floor for warmth from that pot-bellied stove in cold weather. I got to know it even better in a few years when I was old enough to carry coal from our garage on the alley and tote out ashes to spread on the garden. I hated that coal bucket because I was too little in the britches to carry a full load and had to make extra trips. One of Dad's major goals was to keep enough wood and coal in our garage on the alley to keep fires in Mom's cookstove and the pot-belly stove in the living room through the winter. The living room, close to the Warm Morning coal stove was the place to be on cold winter evenings. We played and studied on the floor around the stove and the light from lamp on the stand-table. Dad seldom had the money to buy a battery for the radio but singing and storytelling were great winter activities after homework was finished.

An old pump organ was one of Mom's prized possessions and it sat in a special place in the living room against a wall farthest from the stove. The organ was fascinating with all its keys, knobs (stops) and a three-legged stool with a spiral adjustable seat which provided a lot of 'rides' for kids. We had no radio but family singing was a great winter activity. We three kids would gather around the pump organ for hymns and favorite songs as Mom led the singing. She loved the old church songs and happily pumped away on the pedals when we joined her in family sing-a-longs. Dad never sang with us, he said he didn't like singing, but Mom said it was because he couldn't carry a tune in a bushel basket!

I signed up for free piano lessons in the fifth grade at school and practiced faithfully on the pump organ, but after a few week the music teacher decided I needed a piano to take lessons. My musical career was over, I'm afraid I inherited Dad's lack of talent. An ironic twist is that my son-in-law played the huge Holloway pipe organ in our Presbyterian church for thirty-seven years and I got to sing hymns with an organ.

Firewood

Fall weather brought wood-cutters driving through the neighborhood in with truckloads of wood for sale and they did a brisk business, but Dad had an unending supply of firewood from trees on Grandpa's farm and there was no problem finding a guy with a truck who to help him cut, saw and haul it to town for a share. Their first targets were dead trees already on the ground and small dead limbs for kindling to start fires or feed the kitchen stove. Ash and Poplar and Sassafras timber was light, split easily and was great for Mom's wood-box in the kitchen but our big potbellied stove had a much larger appetite and soft wood simply didn't do the job on cold winter nights. Hardwoods like Oak, Beech and Hickory burned longer and gave off much more heat. I liked the fact that they also left fewer ashes to carry out to spread on the garden. Smoking chimneys from every house in the neighborhood spewed plumes of smoke into the sky all winter and were warmed by cozy heat from nature's bounty.

At the tender age of seven I was included in most Saturday firewood expeditions and sometimes some of the gang went along to help and/or play in the woods Mom packed a lunch of peanut jelly sandwiches, baked sweet potatoes in the skin, a few apples and jugs of water. I was listed as a loading technician and my job was to pick up every stick of wood I could carry and toss it into the truck-bed. Nobody noticed that I took a lot of breaks on the heavy stuff. Axes, saws, sledge hammers and wedges and were the only tools required. Chain saws were years in the future and it usually took two men a full day of muscle and sweat to cut a truckload. Small limbs were whacked ofaf and chopped into proper lengths with an axe while larger limbs had to be sawed off with a one man 'buck saw.' Larger limbs and the trunk called for a six foot cross-cut saw with a man on each end pushing and pulling the long blade through it. The sharp teeth were designed to cut a tree across the grain cut fairly fast and sent curly shavings flying out of the cut once Dad and his buddy got into rhythm. Their last chore was splitting the large sections of the trunk the cut off into small sticks with an axe or wedge and maul. Today, antique saws are in high demand by collectors and new cost two to three hundred dollars. Wood cutting dwindled to few trips to feed the kitchen stove by the time I was old enough to whack trees with an axe. Our woodpile in the woodshed was much smaller after we moved to a better house deeper into Dutchtown and gained a fuel oil stove for the living room.

Grandma's House after Outhouse Days

Several neighborhoods in town did not have access to city water lines or sewers in the 1930's. The city provided town pumps for free water in various sections of town. There was one between 20th and 21st Streets near the Fred Otis house. A dipper or tin can was usually hanging on a town pump for the weary travelers to quench his thirst. Many people walked and needed a cool drink along the way. Some adults carried cups in their purse or pocket. We loved the cool water from a pump on a hot summer day. It came up from the deep underground at about 54 degrees and felt like ice water. The pump was also a dandy place for a guy to soak his head and slick down an unruly head of hair on the way to school. All he needed was a buddy to man the pump handle. It was a great way to cool off in a hurry and improve your looks on a warm school day. Sometime, Mr. Otis' sister Zora would give us bouquets of flowers from her garden to take to our teachers.

The outhouse or 'privy' was a necessary and common fixture in Dutchtown and neighborhoods without access to city sewers. Therefore, many of the homes in our neighborhood had a 'privy' (outhouse), usually a two-hole shack on the alley, as far from the house as possible. There was a general agreement that an outhouse was too near in the summer and too far away in cold winter months. A deep snow really caused family problems. Steamy hot days enriched the outhouse odors and the alley had a certain air about it most of the summer. Some people planted large flower gardens around the privy, hollyhocks did very well, other folks sprinkled the pile of human refuse with lime, but most just left it for the flies and Old Pete to clean out as needed. The old man had a few acres, with a lot of sinkholes, on the edge of town and supplemented his meager farm income by cleaning outhouses. His investment in equipment consisted of a horse and wagon, a shovel, a bag of lime, a bucket, a barrel and a wash tub or two. Pete had a job that most people didn't' want, but he had a fairly steady income, because he had no competition. He was especially busy during the summer months. We kids figured Pete's sense of smell had been numbed years ago, but we felt sorry for his poor old horse.

The days his horse and wagon passed down the alley, everyone in the neighborhood got wind of it. Old Pete was truly a man of distinction!

City alleys were lined with family outhouses of all sizes and shapes. Designs ranged from an unpainted rustic shed to painted vine covered models complete with a flowerbed. They seldom stood alone, but were usually anchored to a garage or barn. A privy had to be well built and able to withstand the rigors of the Halloween season. Pushing over outhouses was a popular although destructive prank of neighborhood teenagers in those days, but one year, the activity backfired on the pranksters. It was a dark and stormy night when young hoodlums tipped over old man Schultz's privy. That's when the trouble started, because Mr. Schultz was sitting in it at the time! The old Dutchman was stone deaf and had no idea that he was under attack until he and the outhouse were tipped over into the alley. Suddenly, it was no longer a Halloween prank and nobody blamed the old man for calling the police. The culprits were charged with property damage and their parents were forced to restore the outhouse to its original condition. Two valuable lessons were learned from this escapade, don't destroy people's property and take a lantern or flashlight when you go to the outhouse any night around Halloween!

A sturdy family outhouse was usually well anchored and expensive to replace and anytime one was pushed over, it was obvious that strong young men were involved. The damage had to be stopped and the neighborhood men met on the porch of Louden's Grocery one evening to organize an alley patrol. The result was men with loaded shotguns walking the neighborhood during October nights. Their shotgun shells were altered by taking out the steel pellet load and replacing it with rock salt. The men did not intend to kill anyone, but any vandal they shot would suffer a long time from salt wounds!

Kids in our gang had a curfew and our parents made sure we kept it so we would not be in the line of fire. Our Halloween devilment was confined to soaping windows, throwing corn and making trick or treat calls at neighborhood houses.

Monkey Business --- The Raridens hired Dad to work in large gas station on the corner of 16th and H Streets just across the street from Grandpa Hutchinson's Saturday parking space. It was a great place to visit because the owners had an unusual drawing card to lure customers. They had a miniature zoo with a cage of monkeys inside the station and a cage with two Black Bears on the corner of their property. The station had a brisk gasoline business and lots of walk-ins to buy a bottle of pop and maybe a few peanuts to feed the monkeys who had learned to beg and show off for visitors. One day I passed too close too their cage and a bony hand reached out and snatched off my brand new aviator cap with goggles. Dad had to go in and fight them to get it back, but I went home bare headed. Mom said I couldn't wear it again until she washed it in kerosene. So that's how I learned that monkeys have lice! The owner later gave the black bears to the city and Bedford maintained a fine bear cage behind the Wilson Park baseball diamond for several years.

Grandma's House --- Maintaining a large family in the poverty of those days was a challenge for young parents. Grandpa had a large family in a small house so in 1913 he decided to build Grandma a 'new house' to ease the crowded conditions of a large family of six boys and two girls in the 'old house'. The four room 'new house' was built on the corner of a crossroads on the Leesville Road just off highway 50 with a wrap-around-porch facing west, north and east. The outhouse, old house, smokehouse and henhouse were in a line on the south facing the yard and pump near the 'new house.' The family continued using the old house several years as a bunkhouse for the boys.

Recently, I accepted my cousin Lisa's invitation to tour the completely renovated Grandma house and discovered that today, the 'new house' is newer than ever and has been featured in several magazines after being restored and by Lisa, who has made it her home.

Touring the house brought many childhood memories of roaming through three rooms of the 'new house 'many times but the fourth room was 'off limits' to rowdy boys. That was the room were Grandma stored her glassware, Victrola Phonograph and records with her collection of pretty things. It was her 'pretties' room' and the closest I ever got to it was standing on the big porch and peeking through the windows!

The porch provided a view of three directions, but the most important was a view of the old house on the right and the barn area. The big barn and farm animals were up the county road beyond the garden. I remember a huge barn with many cow stalls for milking, a vast hayloft and a silo taller than the barn. Corn cribs and a smaller barn for horses, harness, equipment and feed filled out the barnyard area. The farm was blessed with a big cold spring which flowed all year. It was about a hundred yards behind the barn in a little valley. Grandpa and his sons always brought the horses to the barn to cool off before leading them down to the spring. I remember those afternoons when I could get a long ride from Grandpa or one of my uncles.

Hard Times for Kids --- Visiting Grandpa's house and memories of his large family reminded me of Depression times when there were parents with so many children they unable to feed them all. Often, were forced to loan them out to farm families with few or no children to help with farm or housework in return for housing and food. The children were more or less adopted or indentured servants living and working with another family for 'room and board'. This practice of 'farming them out' to work in return for a place to eat and sleep created confusion among families and school officials. Sometimes the children weren't sure which family name to use. Many homeless adults also worked for their 'room and board' to avoid going to the County Poorhouse.

Children across the nation suffered when parents 'farmed them out' to work for other families, offered them for adoption or sold them. Thousands of children ran away from home to live in big cities and existed by menial labor and begging. These 'homeless' kids traveled by trains and became known as 'Boxcar Kids' who rode the rails. Orphans were sometimes sold at auctions and siblings were separated. Some re-united as adults, but others never met again.

The great depression shut down banks and factories. Men wandered the country in search of jobs. The 'Dust Bowl' drought in the West added to the nation's economic problems. Three million families in the South and Great Plains lost their homes by 1937 and homeless families followed the harvest as migrant workers, living in cars, tents and abandoned buildings. Ranchers paid only for the amounts they 'picked' and lured workers with offer of 'free water faucets and firewood at the campsite. Babies, youngsters and adults died from disease, exposure and lack of treatment.

I remember one day when Dad came home and told Mom that a well-to-do farm couple east of town had offered to adopt my little sister, Jean. Mom's reply was quick and loud,

"There are nights we go to bed hungry and the next day isn't any better, but we will never be that desperate and that will never happen!"

There were stretches of time in the winter when jobs were not available and family funds were low. Mom's canned food supply was a blessing and other food supplies were scarce. In those times Mom looked at Dad and said,

"Well, at least the kids can eat, even if we don't."

Dad agreed even though he had a big appetite and in those times Dad would agree, swallow his pride and go ask the Township Trustee for a five dollar 'bean order' to tide us over until the weather improved. My parents were as 'tough as nails' and determined to survive until things got better

Government food surplus aid and school lunch programs provided valuable support and kept our family intact. Help from the Trustee and the Federal Surplus food distribution program was 'iffy' and those sources of help sometimes dried up when they were most needed! Tax funds were limited and it was best to imitate the ants and squirrels and stock up for winter. Food was hard to come by and the flies didn't find many leftovers at our house.

Time softens memories of those desperate early days and I remember them and as happy times when the five of us shared life as a family of two young parents and three scrawny kids. I remember my Mother as a woman who enjoyed life as she scraped, saved and sacrificed to rear three children in the poverty of the Depression. Dad's challenge was to earn enough to 'bring home the bacon' and keep a roof over our heads. Our house was little more than a shack, but my parents met life head-on and lived to enjoy a better life the days after World War II. They are gone now, but live in my memories of those early Depression days on South H Street.

Chapter 2

Leatherwood Creek

Leatherwood Creek has affected my life at one time or another since we moved to a house on the Rariden farm 1n 1929, eighty-seven years ago. The farm's driveway was on the east side of the creek and our route to town was over the old arched Stone Bridge (built for the Cement Plant in the 1896 and up Slaughterhouse Hill. The little creek drains an area northeast of Bedford and is joined by the South Leatherwood branch just south of Highway 50. The clear water runs into Otis Park to add water hazards and beauty to the golf course golf course and Band Shell as it continues along the east edge of Bedford to White River.

The leatherwood plant is a spindly shrub-like tree which grows in rich moist soil in partial shade along creek banks. It has a smooth gray-brown bark and grows to a height of eight to nine feet. The tough, flexible bark and branches were used by Native Americans for weaving, bow strings and fish lines. Early in the Spring it sprouts yellow flowers which turn into oval green leaves. Deer dine on the Leatherwood's buds and it produces red berries in autumn.

Thanks to the generosity of Old Man Glover, Old Man Hyde and the Rariden Brothers who owned the Hilltop Dairy, Leatherwood Creek and much of their land served as a year-round park for Dutchtown children and adults during the poverty of the Great Depression. The city swimming pool and both parks were far across the tracks on the west side of town. Our gang of five, Chad, Doc, Tuffy, Skinny and I, roamed their fields and fished or swam in the cool water of deep holes swimmin' holes on Leatherwood Creek. Sycamore, Clay Banks and Nine Foot, were our favorites. There also were long stretches of shallow water such as Long Hole and Sowbelly for wading, fishing or ice skating. Most eastside kids learned to swim by dog-paddling in the shallow pools, but those were too shallow for good swimmers. We lived in two different houses in Dutchtown during my boyhood and that was a big advantage. We could hike a half mile over the hill to the creek to swim and cool off while sharing the water with fish, crawdads and tadpoles. Sometimes a water snake or frog would show up to give us a target for bean-flipper practice. Often there was a grapevine or rope hanging from a strong limb over the swimmin' hole and we could to swing out like Tarzan of the Apes to drop in the water. There were lots of squeaky Tarzan yells along Leatherwood Creek in those days. Of course, by the time we hiked back up the bluff, we were hotter than we were before we left home!

We also shared the pasture and creek with the large herd of Hilltop Dairy milk cows. The 'red mule' rule was supposed to be followed and we knew to give them the right-of-way along the creek at all times. Some days, we tossed a few rocks their way to 'encourage' them to move on down the creek when they stood in the shallow water above Sycamore to cool off and did what cows do to pollute the water. But usually, we followed the rules and moved back up above them to Clay Banks. It was wiser to follow the advice of Will Rogers who said,

"Always drink upstream from the herd."

But, there were other days when we were too stubborn to move upstream and skinny dipped at Sycamore anyway. We were blissfully ignorant of the terrible disease and contamination risks that would scare us to death today. The cows had to be milked twice a day and were penned in a pasture by the barn at night. They were turned loose after the morning milking to wander down the hill for good grass, water and shade. Ben, the dairy manager, was a real cowboy to us, because he rode Paint, a pretty brown and white pinto horse, to herd the cows back up the hill to the dairy late each afternoon. We begged and pleaded for a ride every time he rode past, but he had no time to waste. However miracles do happen and one afternoon I was late, alone and hurrying to meet the guys at Clay Banks when I met Ben riding Paint coming down to get the cows. He offered me a ride I couldn't refuse and pulled me up behind him. I could almost see the guys turn green with envy when we rode Paint up to the swimmin' hole!

Nine Foot swimming hole was popular with both teenagers and adults because of its depth. Swimmers could wade in from the riffles on a gradual slope, dive from the bank or swing on the grapevine. It became our favorite swimming hole as we grew older because we could dive without scraping knees on the bottom. The gate at the foot of 'I' Street hill was never locked. People often drove in for swimming parties and picnics and the parking area was full on many summer Sundays, especially those days when local churches used it for baptismal ceremonies. We couldn't skinny dip there on most weekends so we or retreated up the crick to Sycamore, but skinny dippin' was sometimes interrupted by girls or families passing by on flower picking expeditions and we had to stay in the water until they were gone. Some Sundays, we wore swimsuits to Nine- Foot and sat in the shade to watch the girls or see the preacher 'dunk' new church members.

Spring was the season Leatherwood served as a marine science lab and we regularly hunted shallow pools and riffles for frogs, tadpoles and crawfish. Tadpoles came in early summer and Doc said we might make some grade points with Mrs. Mudd, our fifth grade teacher, if we took a batch of tadpolees to school for science class. His idea worked and the other kids were fascinated watching our tadpoles grow from slimy egg-shaped ovals with tails to active frogs. Their legs grew out as the tail shrank and slowly disappeared. Mrs. Mudd explained that the tadpoles became frogs by feeding off their tails but we just snickered.

Everybody in our gang knew frogs don't have teeth.

Old Man Hyde

It was the summer of 1935 and the guys in 'our gang of five' were ten years old. Lincoln school was out, we had been buddies since the first grade were ready for adventure. Our neighborhood was on the edge of town and a vacant lot across the alley was all that separated us from the woods and cool spring on Glover's farm. Our favorite fishin' and swimmin' hole was Sycamore in a bend of Leatherwood Creek, only a mile or so away. The 'crick' had turtles, catfish, redeye sunfish, bluegill and suckers in the deeper areas and it was a popular spot to spend some time and maybe catch something to eat. But we had a big problem. The shortest route from our neighborhood was farther south through Old Man Hyde's north field and woods. We called it the 'Forbidden Trail' because the old grouch didn't like trespassers; in fact everyone said it was hard to find anybody he did like! Hyde often said,

"I don't like trespassers on my property!"

The old guy lived alone in a farmhouse big enough for six people and he had posted 'No Trespassing' signs all over his property. His Dutchtown neighbors and kids were smart enough to stay away from his house. Neighborhood gossip had it that there was no welcome mat at his front door, just a hand printed sign that said,

"What the hell are you doing on my porch?"

I guess the old man had good reason to be leery of trespassers because he had chickens, cows, pigs and a big garden. The woods and fields on his place were also ripe with game, nuts and berries. In short, he had most of the things that none of his neighbors had except for one thing; he didn't have a family. People generally agreed that was the reason he was so mean and 'ornery.

The Depression of 1930's was in full swing and all those edible things were tempting targets for the hungry people in the neighborhood. Unemployment was the order of the day and men would work for a dollar a day to put food on the table for their families. It was 1935 before the WPA (Works Project Administration) came along and paid $1.50 a day with steady work. That was considered a good job and $48.00 a month would feed a small family of five, if they didn't eat too much.

There was little serious crime in those days, but it was no surprise that some men resorted to stealing food to feed their family. Chickens were tempting targets. It was so easy to sneak into a henhouse at night, grab a sleeping chicken off the roost, wring its neck, cram it into a burlap sack and vanish into the dark. A police car patrolling neighborhood streets early in the morning was a sure sign a midnight raid had been made on someone's henhouse, or maybe Old Man Hyde had been hit again! So, you see, we all understood why he toted that old double barrel shotgun under his arm any time he was watching and protecting his property. The old man meant business and put up a warning sign on his barn gate:

"NOTICE– ANYONE FOUND IN MY HENHOUSE AT NIGHT — MAY BE FOUND THERE THE NEXT MORNING!

Chad put our fears into words when he said,

"Fellers, if we ain't real careful, we're gonna' get our rear ends full of buckshot"!

We had to be very wary as we sneaked down the path through the woods to Leatherwood creek. In our fertile minds we imagined we were facing an 'armed and dangerous enemy' who spent all day watching for us! Every fishing-swimming trip was a tricky mission because the old guy might be lurking behind one of those big hickory trees in his pasture or a rock down on the steep bluff.

However, our fears didn't stop us, we were determined to take the shortest route to the creek which began near the fence separating the farms of Old Man Glover and Old Man Hyde. (All adults are old when you're a kid). The narrow trail wound through a field of high weeds, into the woods, down over a steep bluff and across a pasture. Needless to say, we kept very quiet while moving down to Leatherwood Creek.

Sycamore, a four foot deep hole in a bend of the creek, was perfect for small kids and fish who loved to swim in the shade of large trees that gave the spot its name. There were bigger and deeper holes along the creek, but Sycamore was best suited for our gang to fish and skinny-dip on those wonderful summer days. Schools of sunfish and bluegill thrived in a deep hole under the tree roots and they loved our bait. We fished the calm water before swimming to avoid scaring away our intended meal. Any fish we caught could be slipped on a stringer and kept in the water until it was time to go home.

The guys in our gang had fishing down to a fine art. We carried fishing gear in our hip pocket. It consisted of a short stick with a hook, line, sinker and bobber wrapped around it. We were prepared to spend a little quiet time fishin' in the shade anytime we were roaming the banks of Leatherwood and saw a fish break water. We traveled light, with our fishing line and sometimes a can of worms for bait. A sharp pocketknife came in handy to cut off a willow branch for a fishing pole and we were in business. We were prepared to throw out hook, line and sinker in record time. Some days we carried a can of fishing worms with us, they would sometimes spoil in hot weather, but bait problem could be solved by catching crayfish under flat rocks in the shallow riffles. Crawdad tails made great bait; just tear them off, strip off the scales and thread the white meat on the hook. In case of a crawfish shortage, we dug for worms on the bank or caught grasshoppers out in the pasture. On a good day, the 'bobbers' (floats) on our lines danced in the water as fish went for our well-baited hooks. I felt like a family hero when fish were biting and I took a mess home for Mom's frying pan.

Joe, "Whatcha' gonna do when the crick goes dry?"
Moe, "Sit on the bank and watch the crawdads die."

Mom could fry up a tasty mess of fish anytime I was lucky enough to bring home a stringer of 'keepers' big enough to eat. We threw back the minnows and fish too small to take home. It was our re-stocking policy to let them grow a little while longer. Sly little minnows could strip a hook with dainty nibbles and steal the bait of the hook without getting caught. You had to be careful when you threaded the worm on the fishhook, too much worm gave fish a chance to eat and run. It paid to pull up your line once in a while to see if you had been robbed. We often tore the worm in half to make it fit. It was sort of a 'fast food' treat for a hungry fish. You had to learn how to fish, the trick was to watch the bobber and jerk the line at the right time. If you did it right, you had another fish to add to your stringer. A quick flick of the wrist was the proper technique. An experienced fisherman would never 'Wabash' a fish. That was a term we used when a greenhorn got excited and jerked the fish out of the water so hard it flew over his head and smacked on the ground behind him.

"There's nothing more relaxing on a summer day than sitting on a shady bank with a fishin' pole in your hand and a keen eye on the 'bobber'. At that point, you realize that you're havin' a really good time, whether the fish are biting or not!"

Men often fished Leatherwood at night and we could spot the best fishing holes by the dead ashes from their campfires. Leatherwood creek flowed into White River a few miles south of town. The river provided excellent perch and catfish fishing for men with Jon-boats. They could put out 'trotlines' and run them daily. River perch and catfish fed many families and provided extra cash for hardworking trotline fishermen during the Depression. Of course, this was years ago before the pollution problems we have today. Fishing provided recreation and free food for the table.

Moe: "Hey Joe, I see you're goin' fishin,' have you got the worms?"

Joe: "Well, Doc says I does, but I'm goin' fishin' anyway!"

Swimming came after the fishing expedition ended and no swimsuits were involved. It was simply a matter of peeling off what few duds we were wearing and jumping into the cool waters of Sycamore. Skinny dipping was a refreshing way to top off the day before we headed back up the 'Forbidden Trail.'

The fishing had been great all summer and we managed to avoid Old Man Hyde by using all our scouting skills sneaking to the creek and back home. However, it all exploded one day in late August when we were on our way home. I was in the lead as we crossed the pasture and started up the bluff when the roaring blast of a shotgun shattered the stillness! Every kid instantly hit the dirt to crawl behind a tree or boulder. Tuffy signaled for me to stay down and play dead. Doc relayed the signal back to Chad and Skinny. We all hugged the ground and the bluff became as silent as a tomb that hot August afternoon. We were terrified and really believed we were in mortal danger from Old Man Hyde's shotgun. We were convinced he had us in his gun sights and we were doomed. Eventually, we realized there were three choices of action: sit tight and wait, run back down to the creek, or go up the hill. Before we made a decision, the silence was broken by a long loud moan up the trail ahead of us! Someone was in trouble and we were afraid to move. Then there were more moans. Chad and Skinny were farthest down the hill behind a big boulder. They motioned and whispered for everybody to creep back down to their position. We crawled and slid down on our bellies until we were safely behind the boulder. It was great to be able to sit up again. We decided we had not been Hyde's target after all, evidently he had shot somebody else, but who? Our choice had been made and we decided to separate and sneak up the bluff to find out who was hurt. It was a dangerous mission, because we had to beware of the enemy while trying to find his victim. However, we all agreed it had to be done, someone needed help!

Anyone who spotted Hyde was to retreat and give our secret Hoot Owl signal, which meant 'stop and drop'. The guy who found the moaner was to give our secret whistle of the Whippoorwill if the coast was clear. (We never considered the fact that both were night birds). Doc took the lead and we spread out to begin slowly creeping up the bluff. It wasn't too long until we heard the call of the Whippoorwill. Doc was standing and giving the 'hurry up' signal by pumping his arm up and down, while pointing toward a grove of Hickory trees. Doc led us in a scramble through the brush into the trees to the right of the trail. Old man Hyde was nowhere in sight, but we were scared stiff as we gathered around a moaning man lying face down behind a log. Who was it and how badly was he hurt? Both questions were answered in a jiffy when he rolled over, sat up, grabbed his bloody leg and yelled,

"Well, don't just stand there gawking like ninnies. Git out of here and find me some help!"

It was Old Man Hyde! He had been hunting squirrels, tripped over the log and shot himself in the leg. Tuffy, Doc and Skinny ran to find help while me and Chad stayed with the old man to help him take off his shirt, rip it to strips and wrap his leg to stop the bleeding. It seemed like forever before Tuffy's dad came down through the trees in his Model A truck to take the bleeding man to the hospital. To make a long story short, Old Man Hyde was in a pickle, because he knew he would be laid up for a while and couldn't do his gardening or chores. That summer we saw a strange thing happen; the folks in the neighborhood pitched in to help him out. They tended his garden, fed the chickens, gathered eggs, milked the cow and generally took care of the farm for a few weeks. Women carried in hot meals until his leg got better and he could get around in the kitchen. Our gang took turns cutting the yard with his old roller lawn mower and doing chores we could handle. It turned out that the hunting accident gave Old Man Hyde more than just a limp. He learned to appreciate his neighbors, took down his No Trespassing signs and put aside a plot of land for a neighborhood garden next summer. He said it was okay for neighbors to hunt in his fields or woods and the Forbidden Trail was open to go down to Leatherwood Creek.

The old man was really thankful our gang had rescued him in the woods and helped around the farm. He bought new shoes for all five of us when school started. Tuffy said it was the first time he ever had a pair of new shoes, because he always wore 'hand-me-downs' from his older brother. Hyde went to Sycamore and fished with us a few times when he was able, but he wasn't much of a fisherman, every time he caught a fish, he Wabashed it!

We all agreed, life was sure a lot easier after Mr. Hyde became our friend and he could go fishing with us anytime!

It just goes to show, anybody can change, even Old Man Hyde!

Hunting for Shade 1934

Summer was our favorite season and school kids waited impatiently for spring rains to pass. May was a month of anticipation and June was our reward. We had endured cold winters and rainy days and were ready for the warm days of summer. Pale kids were tired of staying indoors at home and school. Spring meant 'barefoot days', and every kid in the neighborhood welcomed the warm weather. Kids could hardly wait to shed their socks and shoes and parents were happy because it saved shoe leather. Summer vacation was our time to run barefoot and many did just that. Stone bruises and cut toes were a small price to pay for freedom to run through grass, dirt and mud puddles. The soles of our feet were as tough as leather by the end of summer. School was out until after Labor Day and our three month vacation offered the promise and opportunity of great adventures. We greeted the last day of school with an old chant:

"Schools out, schools out --- Teacher turned the monkeys out."

Many years later I became a teacher and felt exactly the same!

Kids blossomed like daisies in the sunny days of summer vacation when they were free to run and play outdoors. Sunburns usually came first, followed by glowing tans and every guy in our gang was a perfect example of the 'barefoot boy with cheeks of tan.' As the tanning parlors of today say; we had a full body tan! The great outdoors was our playground as we roamed the neighborhood, the woods and banks of Leatherwood Creek. Our dogs loved summer vacation almost as much as kids. My dogs, Collie and Boots, joined the other dogs in our journeys. They were free to trot along with us and nobody ever mentioned a collar or leash. Skinny-dipping in the deep holes of Leatherwood was a great way to beat the heat and almost a daily activity. We started with the dog-paddle and were soon swimming like Tarzan. Parents had mixed emotions about summer vacations. Schools provided a structured order and they knew their children were in classrooms, but summer vacations set their little ones free as birds to roam the neighborhood. I suspect many were happy to see September!

The Shady Spring

Across the alley from our house were the wide fields and woods of Old Man Glover's farm. Mom dearly loved wildflowers and took my little sister and brother on flower-picking trips every spring weekend she found time to take off her apron and escape into the fresh air. Sister Jean's girl friends were always welcome and of course, I was invited to keep an eye on little brother, Kenny. Some of my buddies came along to keep an eye on the girls and the happy group spent several hours in the peaceful valley along the creek. Mom and the girls picked bouquets of spring flowers like violets, kitten britches and buttercups while boys looked for morel mushrooms. Mom saw the area as a park during the 'dog days' of summer when stifling heat was a problem. She would grab a book and take me, my sister and baby brother across the alley to cool off in the shade of a giant oak tree in the pasture. The temperature dropped a few degrees on breezy days and we were happy playing in the dirt under that big oak. Playmates often went along for the shade and summer breezes.

Other humid days, our destination was a grove of large trees in a ravine farther south. The journey ended less than five hundred yards from our house where clear water flowed from under a limestone outcropping into a natural spring of cold water and small pools before it gurgled its way down the hollow toward Leatherwood Creek. The spring was a perfect place to spend a hot afternoon. The deep shade of tall Sycamore and Maple trees surrounding the ravine lowered the temperature several degrees. Wading or splashing in the pools of cool water was a treat to beat the heat. Some days we took sack lunches with peanut butter and jelly sandwiches for a picnic. The cold spring was a great place to cool a jar of our favorite Koolaid.

Of course everybody's dog went along for drinks and a cool spot to flop and snooze. Four or five dogs added to the fun and they scared away any snakes that might be hunting for a cool spot. The sun's rays seldom penetrated the deep shade and the spring was the coolest spot in the neighborhood for kids, dogs and adults on a hot July or August afternoon. However, our little Eden had one flaw which called for a temporary retreat from the spring. Old Man Glover didn't mind our visits to keep cool as long as we gave his four big red mules top priority. Mom called it 'the red mule rule' and everyone in the neighborhood knew to move away from the spring when his mules came down for a drink. The big guys usually loafed in the shade of trees over on the far edge of the pasture where they could keep an eye on the barn in case Mr. Glover brought out some feed, but they headed for the spring when they were thirsty. Our dogs never bothered the mules but they barked to alert us when they heard them coming for a drink and we withdrew to the edge of the ravine. It was exciting to see the thirsty mules come trotting down the dusty path their hooves had carved through the woods.

One section of that path passed under trees our gang often climbed, because that's what boys do. We sometimes sat up there on a limb so low we could almost touch the mules' ears as they passed beneath us. One day out of the blue, Skinny said,

"Hey, I gotta' idea, let's climb a tree and drop down on a mule's back like the cowboys do it in the movies. We'll draw straws to see who goes first!"

We talked it over and decided it was a daring trick we should try, but it had to be a day when we were the only people in the ravine. Such dangerous adventures didn't need any tattle-tales reporting to our parents. I guess it wasn't my day, because I drew the short straw to go first and that made the event much more personal. The big day came sooner than I wanted and I began doubting the wisdom of Skinny's idea. However, we got up the tree and I took the lowest limb to get ready to drop on the last mule. The guys whispered encouragement and advice as the mules came clopping down the path. Thank heavens at the last minute, I thought of a humdinger of an excuse to chicken out.

"Hey guys, I ain't gonna jump on a mule's back without a saddle! Besides, these ain't cowboy horses they're working mules that pull plows and wagons. Who wants to take my place?"

I was answered with complete silence, no one volunteered and I was saved from being branded a coward. More importantly, I had escaped being tossed sky high by a thousand pound mule and maybe getting several broken bones.

Summer Fun

The Carnegie Library was very valuable to us on extra hot days and we made regular visits to browse magazines, check out books and keep cool under the big ceiling fans. Guy who weren't fans of the library had comic books or Big Little books to trade and the Sunday funny papers filled the void. We also had more time for pets ranging from puppies and kittens to a June bug on a string. The primary requirement was that it didn't eat too much. Gold fish and canaries were very popular. Women bred canaries and got a good price for the especially good singers. Many homes had a canary cage next to a window in their living room. Outdoor games were big all summer and there were neighborhood tennis courts, horseshoe pits, and of course basketball goals were nailed a most garages. The baseball fields were in parks across the tracks but in Dutchtown, vacant lots and backyards often became softball fields.

Our big time gambling game was playing marbles in the shade. Most kids had a collection of favorite shooters like 'aggies or steelies.' The steelies were actually ball bearings which could break an opponent's glass marble when used by a player with a strong thumb. The game was much like a 'poor man's pool' for two players. A circle was drawn in the dirt and each boy placed an equal number of marbles in the center and the players took turns shooting to knock marbles out of the circle. Kids often gambled by playing for 'keeps.' Where each shooter keeps the marbles he knocks out of the circle. Gambling generally ended with a lot of crying by the little kids who lost their marbles and the better players having extra marbles to sell or trade at school. However, it was expensive if a tattle-tale 'ratted' on you or a few marbles fell out of your pocket and rattled down the aisle in class. The teacher confiscated all marbles or toys brought to school and usually had a desk drawer full of contraband to hold until summer vacation.

A Barlow knife was also a cherished possession and a coveted item for men and schoolboys. We carried a pocket knife in our britches or overalls for whittling, cleaning fingernails, carving initials on a tree, playing mumble peg or cutting a 'chaw' of tobacco off a plug of Brown Mule. Many men chewed tobacco and brass spittoons were provided in all public buildings such as the courthouse, and absolute necessities in poolrooms and barbershops. Knife trading among the older men loafing under a shade tree was always a possibility. Sometimes, you had to throw in something extra to 'boot' in order to make a deal. Traders might sit and haggle for hours before making a swap, then want to trade back the next day. A guy needed a knife for Mumble Peg which was played with an open knife with handle down and the point held at chin, nose or elbow. The object was to flip the knife so it would stick in the dirt. Games like Tag, Hide and Seek, and King- of- the Hill were popular because they required no equipment.

City officials often approved closing a street for community events of dances, skating parties or sledding, depending on the season. Roller skating was very popular with adults as well as youngsters. Traffic was light and the streets were used as playgrounds for; roller skating, kick –the-Can or sledding. One day a week all summer, the city parks opened the swimming pool across the tracks on the other side of town to give poor kids a free day of swimming really. That wasn't a big deal because most of us didn't have swim suits and Leatherwood swimming holes were much closer.

We competed to win in every sport, but we also learned how to be a good loser. They did not give trophies to everybody. We knew the trophy went to the winners and the losers said, wait 'til the next game. The basic rule of was,simple:

It ain't about whether you win or lose, it's about how you play the game and if you play the game badly, you lose!

Green Apples and Retribution

A majority of Dutchtown homes had seveal fruit trees in the backyard to bolster the family food supply. Apple trees were popular because they ripened at different times during the summer to provided fresh fruit or pies. The timing also allowed time for canning and jars of cooked apples and apple butter provided pies and desert when the trees were cold and bare. Ripe apples could also be wrapped in newspaper and stored for several months. June apples came first as neighborhood trees produced a juicy yellowish green crop which was especially popular with birds, rabbits and boys. All of which visited them eagerly without an invitation. Doc organized the first raid of our fourth grade summer vacation. He led us down the alley behind Grubb's grocery and we sneaked into Dot Brown's backyard for our first taste of fresh apples. It was a wise choice because the old lady walked with a cane and we knew we could escape if she saw us in her trees. Tuffy climbed a tree and threw down enough knobby green apples for all five to stuff our pockets. We almost back in the alley when we heard Dot's shrill voice,

"You boys git out of my trees, I know who you are and I'm gon'na tell your Dads"

We ran on up the alley but her threat shook us up. Me and Skinny wondered if we should take the apples back to her, but we were out-voted. Chad convinced us that she was bluffing and there was no way she could have recognized us that far away. So, we went over to Tuffy's house and found a shady spot to enjoy our first green apples of the summer. They were hard to chew, but a stolen fruit always tasted better, so we devoured all of Dot's green apples until nothing was left but a pile of cores which we later used in a game of 'Apple core -- Baltimore'. Skinny was still worried about Old Dot talking to our parents and he and I were ready to go home and take our medicine. Doc, Chad and Tuffy insisted we were not recognized and said we should all go home for supper acting innocent as lambs. That plan worked because the old woman had not reported our theft. Stealing a few green apples was not considered a major crime but we were always punished if we got caught stealing. Food and their few belongings were very important to families in the Depression, parents had a reputation to protect and discipline was maintained at all cost. However, older and wiser folks knew from experience that if you snitched a few green apples, the crime often provided its own punishment.

The harsh punishment for our crime was delayed but it struck with a vengeance in the dark of night in the form of stomach aches and diarrhea. We paid the full price for stealing. A few days after our recovery, we were walking past Old Dot's house on our way to Grubbs to share a cold bottle of Nehi Orange Crush. She was sitting in her rocker on the front porch, but stood as we passed and yelled to ask ever so sweetly,

"Hello boys! Can you tell me if my apples are ripe yet?"

We instantly knew why she hadn't bothered to call our parents. That old lady knew all along that we would suffer for our crime. For it is written:

"No one escapes the Green Apples' Revenge!

The Iceman

The icebox was a necessity for even the poorest family to save food and left-overs. Ours was an oak cabinet about four feet tall with a hinged lid over a waterproof top compartment which held the block of ice. There were four doors on the front with compartments for storing food and a large drip pan underneath to be emptied daily as ice melted. There weren't many leftovers in those days, but milk and food spoiled quickly on hot summer days and the big ice plant up by the Monon depot had a fleet of ice wagons on city routes all summer. The demand for ice was much less in cold weather, ice didn't melt nearly as fast in cooler kitchens and families often used home-made window boxes. However, the ice company had the weather problem solved, because they also sold coal and used the same horses and wagons to deliver. The milkman came early every morning and like the iceman, there was a card to leave in the window for an order.

Kids along the route kept watch for our ice man, Cat-eye Keen, on hot summer days because of the chance to get free ice chips. He was a very popular guy and one of our favorite deliverymen all summer. I can still see him driving his old white horse hitched to a green ice wagon with orange wheels. His horse knew the route very well and usually stopped in front of the homes of Cat-eye's regular customers. The horse and wagon left the ice plant with a heavy load of blocks of ice covered by a heavy black tarp. Every customer had an ice card to place in a screen door or window to show the iceman what size a block of ice to deliver. It was usually a ten cent order for twenty-five pounds although twelve and a half pound orders were not uncommon on cool days. Cat-eye stopped the horse when saw the sign and uncovered the ice to chip off the correct size block. He wore a leather pad over his back so he could pick up the block of ice with his tongs and tote it on his back to place in the customer's icebox. We were especially blessed at our house, because he stopped at Auggy's for his lunch break. He tied his horse in the shade carried a block of ice in to the ice box, came back with a half bucket of water for his horse and went back to eat his sack lunch in the cool basement. His routine seldom varied and as soon as the coast was clear, we rushed to the back of the wagon, lifted the tarp and passed out ice chips for a free and glorious summer treat! Some days, we had time to use his ice-pick to chip off more ice in case there wasn't enough to go around. Many years later I learned that Auggy usuually had an extra bottle of home brew in the ice box for Cat-eye's lunch break.

It was generally agreed that we enjoyed Cat-eye's lunch break as much as he did on those really hot 'dog days' of summer!

Evening Shade

The stifling heat of August demanded an attitude of, 'Damn the flies and 'skeeters' and full speed ahead! Living in a hot house in mid-summer was nearly impossible without electricity for fans. Our only option was to open the doors, raise every window in the house and hope the screens on doors and windows would let in cool breezes and keep all winged pests out. Dad said he was never sure if we were letting cool air in or hot air out. Screen doors slammed during the day as kids ran in and out and a kid who didn't close the screen door often heard one of Dad's sarcastic remarks:

"Wuz you born in a barn? Close that door, you're lettin' all our flies out!"

The large Maple trees in our backyard were a blessing and valued for their deep shade. There were also fruit trees and a large grape arbor which served double duty. Treeless neighbors often invited themselves over to share our cool and breezy backyard on hot summer nights. Mom and Dad hosted a lot of 'shade tree seminars' on summer evenings and the Kool Aid flowed like wine, providing someone brought the ice. There were also nights when neighbors pooled their resources and had a 'taffy pull' or made a gallon of ice cream. We owned a hand cranked wooden freezer and of course someone had to go to the Ice Plant for a block of ice. I took on that job as soon as I got my bike with a wire basket on the handle bars. Mom poured the ingredients into the steel gallon canister, we packed the freezer with chipped ice and rock salt and took turns cranking until we cold crank no more. Some covered the freezer and let it freeze harder, but we usually skipped that part, pulled out the paddle and dish out the rich desert.

The old folks offered various opinions or solutions to the problems of life in the Depression and of course on the weather. People who owned a radio or subscribed to the newspaper did a lot of the talking. A kid could learn a lot by listening and I soon learned it was wise to heed the old adage, 'children should be seen, not heard,' because it was strictly enforced.

Story telling was a popular form of entertainment in those days long before we had a radio and we heard inventive variations of the same story way too many times. Strangers or anyone with new material were always appreciated and encouraged to share their new material. Reggie, the pushcart man, never had much to say, but sometimes he reported or confirmed fresh news he picked up at one of the stores on his route. My favorite time was when Granny Johnson told stories of growing up in a log cabin in the woods of Martin County during the 1880s. Her tales of wildcats on the cabin roof or wolves howling at the door sent chills up my spine. Then there were stories to warn us about the Gypsies who might come through town anytime. She warned that they would steal chickens, children and anything else that wasn't nailed down. The Gypsies never appeared, but I suspected that some of the parents indulged in wishful thinking about losing their kids for a few days. Sometime, Skinny's Dad would tell a ghost story late in the evening and adapt to our neighborhood surroundings. He scared the daylights out of us kids and his vivid tales sometimes dampened our desire to sleep outside. Several of the mothers weren't too happy about having to escort their kids to the outhouse for several nights after one of his scary whoppers.

Listening to stories, playing 'hide and seek' or catching a jar full of lightning bugs were things to do in the dark. (Mom made us set them free before bedtime.)

Some nights we spread a pallet and slept on the floor near the front door or out on the roofless porch. Other times, kids in the gang came over and we camped out in the front yard. Pitching a 'bed-sheet tent' under the stars was a great adventure, but we paid a price for keeping cool. Our little bodies provided a source of fresh blood for the skeeters, ticks and chiggers and they welcomed us like hobos at a smorgasbord.

Those chigger bites would itch for a week. The best treatment was to rub a mixture of lard and salt on the spot where the mite burrowed into your skin. Ticks were more visible and the little bloodsuckers could be picked off with tweezers and nobody ever heard of lyme disease. Chiggers were detested pests without friends, but entomologist, H.B. Hungerford, wrote a limerick in their honor.

The thing called a chigger -- Is really no bigger Than the smaller end of a pin, -- But the bump that it raises -Just itches like blazes -- And that's where the rub sets in!

My dogs, Collie and Boots and the other guys' dogs, often crawled inside or curled up by our tent and we appreciated their company. A few fleas just added to our camping adventure in the wilds of our yard and we figured dogs were great protection from ghosts and Gypsies in those hot Hoosier nights of the Great Depression!

We didn't have much of a house, in the early years of the Great Depression, but we had a heck of a backyard for the steamy nights of Hoosier summers!

Chapter 3

Gardens and Canning

Hunger was a real problem in the depression and summer offered the opportunity to plant, harvest and preserve food for winter days. More food was available in the summer months, but we never fattened up because we were so active. Dad farmed our large backyard garden and rented several nearby vacant lots by giving the homeowner a share of his harvest. He spaded the small plots with his long handled shovel and hired Old Pete to plow the bigger ones. Pete cleaned outhouses, but was always ready to bring over his horse and plow to make a few bucks plowing gardens. Dad planted lot of potatoes, yams and dry beans for the winter months. Canned corn, green beans, tomatoes, beets and potatoes for the cellar was our main goal and I got in on most of the planting, hoeing and weeding those gardens all summer. Weeding the gardens wasn't too bad, I became pretty good wielding a hoe and had calluses on my hands to prove it. The one job I hated most, was killing bean and 'tater bugs'. Dad couldn't afford to put out money for 'bug dust' (insecticides) so we did it the old fashioned way. Kenny, Jean, and I spent a lot of hours crawling up one row and down the other with a tin can half full of 'coal oil' (kerosene). Our job was the same, whether the prey was bean beetles or tater bugs; pick off the little devils and baptize them in the can! They were eating leaves off our food and had to die! Dad said it was us or them, so thousands of bugs bit the dust every summer. I could never understand why Noah let those garden pests board the Ark!

Canning fruits and vegetables was a necessary summer task to preserve Dad's garden harvest. We ate well from the garden all summer, but Mom washed up the Mason or Ball glass jars, bought new lids and canned as much as possible. It was food we needed for the long winter months and storing a food supply was essential. She stored a large supply and every jar we emptied in the winter was washed and put away for the next summer

Canning was a family project with chores for everyone and on many summer mornings, our kitchen became a food preservation laboratory. Me, my little sister Jean and brother Kenny helped out with washing vegetables, shucking corn, stringing and snapping the green beans. One of my favorite tasks was peeling peaches, because I could eat a piece once in a while. One canning processes involved the hot kitchen stove covered by a large copper boiler full of sealed Mason glass jars of green beans cooking in the jar (cold packed.) Stewed tomatoes went into tin cans with a lid which had to be sealed with hot red wax! Needless to say, we had our own sauna during the canning season. Families could sometimes get a five dollar food certificate for groceries from the Township Trustee, we called them 'bean orders'. That aid and the federal surplus food distribution program were 'iffy' and those sources of help sometimes dried up when they were most needed! Tax funds were limited and it was best to imitate the ants and squirrels and stock up for winter. We cleaned our plates at every meal and the flies didn't find many leftovers at our house.

The federal government set up programs to provide surplus foods for needy families. Lawrence County had almost a fourth of families on relief. People across the nation stood in long lines to receive rations of food based on family size. Dried beans, rice, flour, canned beef, peanut butter, and grapefruit were among food items distributed to help families survive. The program was a great benefit to our family. However, the flour sometimes had weevils in it, so I fed it to my chickens. They loved the extra meat and their eggs never had weevils. There was also a program to allow Bedford Dairy to distribute free milk once a week. Dad was working and Mom was canning in the summer of my fifth grade. We had to bring our own container, so I stood in line one day a week to carry home a gallon Karo syrup bucket full of free milk. Mom rationed it to make great breakfasts of biscuits and gravy and when we ran out of milk, we had 'water gravy' with our meals. Dried beans were a main part of our diet and a low cost item at any grocery. A large pot of Great Northern beans flavored with a chunk of bacon (sow belly) could feed a family of five for lunch and supper.

They were delicious with cornbread and buttermilk and provided our main source of protein. It is still one of my favorite meals. Most families kept a pot of beans warming on the back of the cook-stove all day.

Beans were so common that they were included in our vocabulary. We said a fibber was 'full of beans,' a tattler 'spilled the beans, and a five dollar food stamp issued by the Township Trustee was dubbed a 'bean order'. If you had a good idea, they said, 'that's using the old bean'. We even had a poem for beans.

Beans, beans the musical fruit ---- The more you eat the more you poop!
The more you poop the better you feel ---- So let's have beans for every meal.

Nature's Bounty

Fishing and hunting were important sources of food. Hunger was a reality and putting food on the table was a definite challenge. People became very creative in finding ways to add to their family's meager diets. Victory gardens sprouted in backyards and vacant lots all over the neighborhood. A high percentage of town yards had fruit trees and much of household food was home-grown during the Depression and WW II years. Dieting was not a problem and there were very few overweight people in our end of town. The Monon railroad ran through the town square and the well-to do folks lived on the west side of town. Our Dutchtown neighborhood in the southeast section of town was literally on the wrong side of the tracks! However, living on the edge of town provided opportunities to gather nature's bounty from the nearby fields, streams and woods and practically every man had fishing gear and a shotgun for hunting. We hunted, fished and scrounged for food wherever we could find it! Squirrels, rabbits or fish often provided meat for the table. Our family never dined on possum or raccoon, but many people feasted on roasted or barbequed coon during the depression, it beat starving. Possum meat was too greasy but that was probably before 'Possum Helper' came on the market.

Hunting was one way to add meat to the meager diets of depression families. Rabbits, squirrels, 'possums, groundhogs and raccoons were considered edible in those days and were fair game when 'huntin' season' opened. However, the legal hunting season was ignored by unemployed men who hunted to feed their hungry kids. They seldom bought a license and took their chances on evading the game warden. Legally they were 'poachers' but actually they were just desperate. We hunted rabbits in the fields and edge of the woods and the results were best when you had a good rabbit dog. Doc's Dad had a beagle hound that was a great rabbit dog. Old Sport, wasn't much to look at, but the sad-eyed dog was a ball of fire on a hunt. He would jump a rabbit and chase it around in a circle until it came back past us so we could get a shot at it. You could waste a lot of time and miss 'jumping' a lot of rabbits unless you had an expert like Old Sport on the job. Once he put his nose to the ground, you had a tail wagging buddy who could sniff 'Brer Rabbit out of any briar patch.

The fields and woods were crowded with hungry hunters in those days and there were sometimes gunshot injuries or fatal accidents. Many of those accidents were caused by carelessness, some men shot at anything that moved in the brush. Our Dads told us to come home on days the woods were full of hunters.

Hunting squirrels in the woods was a quiet early morning activity when squirrels were eating. We planned our hunts so each of us had an assigned section and agreed to never fire at a squirrel on the ground. We spread out in the woods before sunrise, found a comfortable seat under a nut tree and waited for the squirrels to come swinging through the trees for breakfast. We had to be motionless until they began 'cutting nuts' and bits of hulls came raining down through the leaves. Then a guy could quietly sneak into position to get off a good shot or two before they fled the scene. Once the shotgun blast shattered the stillness, the hunter had two choices. He could sit down and enjoy the serenity of an early morning in the woods to wait for their return or sneak quietly along to another tree where they were cutting. Southern Indiana had many beautiful woods with extremely tall trees seventy years ago. One hunter complained that he hunted in trees so tall that the buckshot from his sixteen gauge shotgun couldn't reach squirrels in the treetops. His tale was topped by another guy who said he had to put rock salt in his shells to keep the meat from spoiling before it hit the ground. As the old saying goes, the first liar doesn't have a chance! Good hunters bragged of using a .22 rifle to 'bark' the critters out of the tree but had to be a sharpshooter to bring home a mess of squirrels with a rifle. At the age of fourteen, I was content with my Stevens single barrel twelve gauge shotgun with a shot pattern about the size of a basketball. It gave me a better chance of knocking a squirrel out of a treetop or hitting the rabbit as he whizzed past. Of course, if I hit either too well, there wasn't much left and we did spit a lot of buckshot into the plate when we sat down to enjoy one of Mom's fried rabbit or squirrel dinners. Hunting put meat on the table, but shells were costly (ten cents) and a hunter's goal was to bag enough game to feed his family and have extra game to sell for cash to buy more shells. Men who skinned out a rabbit to sell left the fur on one back foot to show that it was really a rabbit. Some guys had been selling skinned cats!

My buddies and I had a couple of close calls in those pre-war years. Hunting in groups was serious business and you had to be on your toes when everybody was carrying a deadly weapon. Our closest call to a fatality came one November day when we were teenagers. The five of us were rabbit hunting on the deserted Mullins farm when a cold rain came up and we ran to an old barn to keep dry. Time dragged on that afternoon and a couple of the guys in the corner got to 'horsin' around and a shotgun went off accidently. The full load went between me and Tuffy! The buckshot cut a belt loop off his jeans, scared the stuffins' out of me and blew a hole the size of a basketball through the side of that old barn!

No one said a word, but by the time the echo of the blast died down, each kid had unloaded his gun and silently stepped out into the cold rain to head home for a warm fire and safety. Getting wet was the least of our worries and that day was the end of group rabbit hunting by the Dutchtown Gang.

Springtime we hunted for mushrooms, dandelion greens, poke and other greens. Boiled Sassafras tree root made excellent tea. Summer was berry-picking time and we picked gallons of wild blackberries and raspberries in fields near and far. I favored the blackberry patches because you could stand and pick several vines. Most berry patches were well trampled down and picked clean, but the briars reproduced and the trick was to get back when the new crop ripened. We went on distant trips if Dad could find a buddy with a car and had funds to help pay for the gas. We loaded the car with buckets and five gallon cans to spend hours in the 'boonies' picking plump berries and enduring the hot sun. Blackberries were great for a good pie and we canned many pint jars of jam and jelly for special treats on days when the frost was on the pumpkin or snow was on the roof. It helped to think of those things as you sweated and got sun-burned. We wore long sleeved shirts and hats to avoid the pesky briars reaching out to scratch us. It was wise to be on the lookout for copperheads and rattlesnakes when trampling down thick weeds to reach the thorny berry briars. Pickers had to battle 'chiggers', those teeny little red mites that burrowed under the skin and itched like the dickens for a few days. The best protection was to tie a strip of cloth soaked in coal oil (kerosene) around your ankles before you went on a berry-picking expedition. Of course the chiggers always won and the best treatment was a mixture of lard and salt dabbed on the bite and a lot of scratching.

Fall and cool weather was the time for hunting walnuts, butternuts, and hickory nuts. They were great winter snacks for cracking around the stove on cold winter evenings. We cracked them with a hammer on a sad iron and threw hulls in the stove. Our gang was in the walnut business for a couple of years and we had a few good customers who would pay two bits for a bushel. That was only a profit of ten cents each, but we gave it a try. Successful walnut hunters were easily identified by their stained hands. It took weeks to wear off and our brown hands were very prominent in our Lincoln School sixth grade class photo. Walnuts were free when they fell from trees early in the Fall but there was a lot of work to do before we had cash in our hands. We had to find the trees in the woods, pick up, hull-out and carry them home in a grass sack. Skinny and Tuffy went right after school one day and stain ruined their good shirts. Our garage roof was low and flat enough to spread the hulled nuts out to dry, but it was two weeks before we gathered a bushel to sell for that magnificent sum of two bits (half dollar) a bushel. It took an awful lot of walnuts fill a bushel basket, so we quit the business and looked for easier ways to make a dime!

We tried gathering persimmons and paw paws (Indiana bananas) to sell, but we had to beat the possums and other varmints to the trees and seldom won because they worked day and night. Many days I found enough ripe persimmons on the ground to gather and take home for Mom to bake a wonderful pudding. The persimmon is a novelty because the trees only grow in a very small area of the mid-west. Our neighboring city, Mitchell, Indiana hosts a week long Persimmon Festival each September featuring pudding contests. The rare pudding is often on the menu at nearby Spring Mill State Park. However, a word to the wise, never eat a green persimmon for your mouth will pucker up so tight you can't whistle. Every guy in our gang can testify to that from firsthand experience. You really need to know what you're doing when you mess around with a green persimmon.

The Great Skinny-dip Caper

Our gang roamed the banks of Leatherwood creek all summer of our fifth grade and skinny dipping at Sycamore, our favorite swimming hole, was the order of the day. The big trees on the bank allowed us swim in shade or full sun. There were a few precautions to take when swimming in our 'birthday suits.' We had to be careful where we stashed our clothes because some guys might sneak up and hide them, tie them in knots or fill pants pockets with rocks and toss them in the creek. Our security plan was simple. We wadded the riffles below the deep water, stripped down on the bank opposite the trees and relied on our dogs to sound the alarm if anyone came around. The system failed one day in late July and led to an embarrassing incident for our gang.

Maudy Harkins and four other girls in our Lincoln School fifth grade class caught us skinny dippin' at high noon. We knew something was up the minute we saw them because they were on our side of the creek. The dogs hadn't warned us and that fact was really worrisome. Doc said we might as well get ready for trouble, because we had teased them a lot during the past year. We didn't have to wait long for the bad news. Maudy led the jeering as they bragged about sneaking up on us while we were splashing around in a water fight and tossing our pants into a weed patch in the gravel several feet from the water. After that announcement, they splashed across the shallow riffles and sat on the bank, laughing and daring us to come out and find our duds. Maudy and her gang had made themselves comfortable and showed no signs of leaving. They were having a fine time at our expense. Now, the tables were turned and we were their helpless victims. We had been ambushed, caught like rats in a trap and doomed to endure jeers and shrill catcalls like:

"Come on out boys we won't peek"

Chad called for a quick huddle and we decided to stay in the creek until our tormentors got tired of the game and went on their merry way. However, the 'pests' enjoyed the sunshine and continued taunting us! The day dragged on and they showed no signs of leaving for lunch. The duel of minds continued and time ebbed as slowly as the current of the creek. We began to realize that we had teased them too often and they weren't about to release us from their trap. It was evident that Maudy's gang had been working on the project for weeks and we were the victims of very clever planning by girls determined to get revenge for jokes and 'cat calls' we had personalized and thrown at them during school recess! Little things like:

"Maudy Rose all dressed in black – Maudy Rose sat on a tack – – Maudy ROSE!" or point out anyone of them and chant, "Dirty Lil, Dirty Lil --- She lives up on Garbage Hill --- never took a bath and never will! --- Hock putt, Dirty Lil."

We were tired of soaking, but there was one puzzle to solve before we gave up. Something was fishy, why didn't our dogs warn us when the girls were stealing our clothes? Tuffy was elected to yell and ask Maudy that burning question,

"Hey Maudy, why didn't our dogs bark when you guys swiped our clothes?"

She just laughed and replied,

"Oh that was easy, we've been tossing them treats when we passed your houses for the last three weeks. Today, we were just their friends tossing them more treats. Wait, I'll show you!"

With that, she gave a loud whistle and our 'loyal' dogs bound out the shade and splashed across the riffles to join the tormentors on the other side off the creek for more treats. That demonstration crushed our morale and all hopes of redemption. We finally realized why our strategy wasn't working. The sun was slowly sinking in the west, skinny-dippin' had lost its charm and we were water-logged. Chad said we should ask for a truce and make one more try for a deal before we surrendered and waded out to find our clothes. We all agreed he could do the talking. So, he told Maudy and the girls we were sorry and ask them to please leave and let us get to our clothes. The giggling girls held a brief discussion and after some arguing, they agreed to let us save our dignity. They promised to put their hands over their eyes while we came out to get our pants.

It wasn't much of a deal, but we were water-logged. Skinny said he didn't believe them and decided to stay in the water. The rest of us took them at their word, which was another mistake! Chad counted to three, before we splashed out of the water 'buck naked' and raced across the hot creek gravel into the weeds for our pants. All the while, the girls were laughing and cheering us on in our race and search for decency. I threw Skinny his pants and took off after the girls, but it was no use they were on the other side of the crick and had too much of a head-start. They made a clean escape up the trail at top speed. Later, Skinny said they kept their promise to keep hands over their eyes, but were peeking through their fingers as we scrambled to put on our duds!

Our gang patrolled Leatherwood creek in the final days of summer hoping to catch the girls wading, but we never did! We had faint hopes they might keep quiet about the event, but we should have known better. School started after Labor Day and Maudy and her gang bragged to every kid in Lincoln school. News of their victory with the 'Great Skinny Dip Caper' had been spread far and wide. Our gang had to endure teasing, smug looks and giggles until the story became old news. There was nothing we could do about our humiliation, but laugh it off. We had literally been caught with our pants down and just had to grin and 'bear' it.

But of course, we had already done that!

Reggie's Push Cart

Reggie was a little old man who lived, or rather existed, in two back rooms of the big old Johnson house down the alley behind our house. He was a push–cart man who eked out a few bucks a week by cleaning stores and hauling away trash and outdated food discarded by grocers. Mrs. Johnson's husband didn't come home from the first World War. People said he died in the trenches in France and widow Johnson was just a notch above being homeless herself. Hard times call for hard decisions and the old couple shared separate sections of the house with the community's blessing. To me, they seemed a perfect fit for the dilapidated old house which had also endured many hard years of neglect.

Reggie was the proud owner of a big two wheeled push-cart which he used in his business. The heavy cart with iron wheels from some farm vehicle looked too heavy for the small man, but he managed it very well. He said his secret was dabbing lots of grease on the axle. They called it a push-cart, but he pulled it most of the time. The hilly streets of South 'H' Street were a challenge, but he had a line for that.

"I push when it's empty and pull when it's full and the street is downhill most of the way home."

The old man usually had a smile and wave for us when he stepped between the cart's handles and bent forward to push his heavy cart up the street. Sometimes, to amuse us, he would slap his legs with one hand and gallop like a horse. Some folks said the he was not playing with a full deck, but Dad said he had properly been shell-shocked in the war and just doing his best to eke out a living and get along in hard times.

Everyone in the neighborhood knew when Reggie headed for town, it was usually about the time we had to go to school. Our dogs were out to see us off so they included Reggie in the celebration before they went back to sleep. He enjoyed the attention as the barking pack escorted him up the street but Chubby's dog, Brutus, worried him. Brutus was an impressive canine; the biggest dog in the neighborhood with a full set of teeth. The old man once said to Dad,

"Clyde, I'm a little bit leery of that big surly Brutus, do you think he would ever bite a feller? I don't like the way he looks at me."

He was satisfied when Dad told him the big dog was gentle and his bark was worse than his bite. Our dogs really made a racket when Reggie did his horse imitation and galloped with his cart. Things got quieter when we chased them back home and started our four block walk up the street to classrooms in old Lincoln School on the corner of 20th and 'H' Streets.

Weekends and summer mornings, we slept-in, kept our dogs quiet and Reggie moved out quietly. Four or five days a week, weather permitting, he navigated his heavy cart up the street and into the alleys behind various stores. There were several other push-cart operators in our small town during the Depression and competition for work was keen. Some patrolled the town's alleys to pick up discarded items they could sell at the junkyard, but Reggie had a clientele of grocers who hired him because he was a veteran and a good worker, plus the fact that he was dependable and clean. He worked cheaply because he had a small income on the side! Grocers had no refrigeration and they used large 'ice-boxes' to cool meat, fruits and vegetables. Those items aged quickly and had to be discarded and Reggie pushed or pulled his cart to those stores on a regular schedule to haul away trash and/or food no longer fit to sell. He kept the trash and food in separate containers because he had a ready market for much of the out-dated fruit and vegetables. He hauled it back to the south end of Dutchtown where housewives of down and out depression families waited to check-out his harvest of the day. The old veteran made a few extra bucks and everyone benefited when he had a good day. Women were willing to pay a few cents for fruits or vegetables which could be salvaged for their kitchen. Careful cleaning and trimming produced edible food for the family table. Mom was one of his regular customers and I remember bruised fruit, brown bananas, soft oranges, stale bread, old potatoes and best of all, outdated chocolate candy, turned white and hard as a rock! Reggie's prices were very reasonable and he was pleased to be accepted as a member of the community. He dumped his un-usable trash in a sinkhole across the alley to burn when the wind was calm. Chad said he was five before he found out bananas were yellow!

Neighborhood kids and dogs liked Reggie and we were glad that kindhearted old Widow Johnson rented him a room in the back of her house. He also had the use of a small woodshed to store the cart and keep kindling firewood and coal dry. No money was involved in the arrangement. Reggie got a place to live and two meals a day in exchange for bringing in discarded food and doing a few chores around the house. He kept the wood-box and water buckets full and like most of the neighbors, he carried water from the town pump on the corner. In return, the old lady washed his clothes, soiled from hard work and lack of a large wardrobe. Mrs. Johnson usually had a shirt and pair of bib overalls drying on the clothesline across his porch. She hung them in his room behind the stove in wintry weather.

Reggie's most important winter chores were chopping wood, keeping the fires going in two stoves and carrying out the ashes. On snow days, he shoveled a clear path to the outhouse down on the alley. Summer evenings our gang sometimes went down to visit him and sit in the yard to hear his WW I stories. We were never invited inside the old house, but one day I sneaked a peek into his room. There wasn't much to see, just a small stove for heat and warming food, table, chair, small cot in the corner and a dry sink with a water bucket and dipper. He had a bench on the small back porch for loafing and whittling on rainy days. The old veteran had a lot of stories about his days in the war when he was a 'Doughboy' fighting in the trenches in France. Of course he often came up to our house for the evening 'shade tree seminars.' His stories were exciting oral history lessons in the old days when few families had radios and nobody even imagined a thing called television. To us, it was just a make-believe gadget we saw in the Buck Rogers or Flash Gordon movies of the Saturday movie matinees.

Reggie worked hard to make the best of life in a tough world.

The Mom and Pop Grocery

There were seventy-five independent groceries in our small town when I was a kid in the 1930's. I recall the names and location of many those in our Dutchtown neighborhood. There were sometimes two in the same block. The small stores were business ventures to earn a living during the Depression and usually operated by a man and his wife who had living quarters or a sitting room in the rear for a place to relax during slack periods. A jangling bell on the door alerted them when a customer entered the store.

Grocery 1942 --- note the prices Library of Congress

I remember many of those people who sold me penny candy, jawbreakers, Nehi pop and Eskimo Pies. Some of the grocery names were Grubb, Hancock, Fields, Stipp, Bridwell, Garrison, Endris, Louden and Jingo's Meat Market. Profits were slim and a kid with a few pennies was treated as an important customer. Mrs. Grubb's grocery was near our house and she had a glass enclosed penny peg board game mounted below the candy counter. It had slots with values of one, two or three cents at the bottom and we would drop a penny in the top, hold our breath and watch it rattle down the metal pegs. Every kid had a chance to double or triple his money at the bottom. It was a great sales gimmick and exciting to watch your penny bounce down toward a prize. Now the pegboard had your penny and Mrs. Grubb handed out your choice of candy. It was a win-win situation because you never lost the value of your penny, but you could count on one hand the number times you won!

Few men could afford cars and most walked or hitched a ride to their job. Taxi fare was ten cents to any place in town, but who could afford that when you were working for peanuts? Chubby's mother worked at the Reliance shirt factory almost a mile from their house and she walked to and from work five days a week. She saved a dollar a week and got lots of fresh air and exercise. I often carried Dad's lunchbox to him when his WPA job was in our neighborhood. The usual contents were a small can of pork and beans, can opener, spoon and two cold biscuits. His monthly WPA earnings of forty eight dollars bought a lot of groceries in those days. The average annual income in 1935 was less than $1,200. Prices were low and five dollars would buy several large sacks of groceries; hamburger was about forty cents a pound, peanut butter, baloney was twenty-five cents a pound and you could mail a letter with a three cent stamp. Housewives walked to the nearest store that would give them credit. Grocers often gave credit by allowing a customers to 'run a bill' until payday. They had to be wary of being swindled, but many of those trusting souls just couldn't say no to a family with hungry children. Extending credit was risky business because some families would run up a grocery bill and move away. A few were forced out of business from allowing too much credit. Jingo's Meat Market had been 'stung' so many times that he put a large sign above his meat locker, which read:

"Cash to all --- Credit to none ---I love you all — But I need the mon"

Families who owned homes were a much better credit risk. Dad managed to run a bill at King's grocery across town on Washington Avenue near Wilson Park. Gas was thirteen cents a gallon and they offered home delivery. Candy treats for the kids were included when

Dad paid the 'bill.' It was just like Christmas, we never knew what we would get until the black 1934 Ford panel truck arrived! I applied for credit one hot July day when Chad were at the park and with a terrible thirst and in desperate need of a couple bottles of cold Nehi Orange Crush pop. I wandered into King's grocery and asked to put a dime on Dad's bill, my request was quickly and coldly denied, only Dad could buy on the bill.

Store-bought 'victuals' were dry foods or materials for 'home cooking' and those items were sacked or wrapped and weighed by a clerk before being handed across the counter to the customer. Families bought few canned or packaged goods in those days, most meals were prepared from 'scratch' and cooked on the kitchen stove. Grocers used lots of sacks, paper trays, wrapping paper and string when waiting on customers. Lard and peanut butter was hand-dipped from a large container, slapped into a tray, wrapped in paper and tied with string. Mom usually handled the wrapping. An order for hamburger was handled the same way. Pop weighed the meat, chopped it up and fed it into the hand cranked meat grinder while the customer watched and waited. Baloney or minced meat (as we called it) was sliced on a hand-cranked slicer, weighed and wrapped. The grocery couldn't have operated without a good set of scales and a large roll of string and wrapping paper. Fruit and dry items were put in sacks and flour, dry beans and cornmeal was often sold in ten pound bags. Mothers baked a lot of biscuits and cornbread and a loaf of store-bought white bread was a rare family treat.

Stores sold kerosene (coal oil) which was stored in a barrel outside the store. It cost five cents a gallon and I remember many errands to fill our old tin coal-oil bucket which had a potato jammed on the spout to replace a lost cap. Many homes used kerosene for lamps and four-burner kitchen stoves. The stove had a bracket on the end to hold a gallon bottle. The trick was to fill the bottle with coal-oil and quickly up-end it into the bracket. Gravity allowed the kerosene to flow down a pipe to braided cloth 'wicks' on each burner. Wicks soaked up the oil and when the housewife wanted to cook, she turned up the wick to light it with a wooden match. Matches were used a lot in those old 'kerosene days', in fact, most kitchens had a special holder mounted on the wall to hold a brick-sized box of matches to be used as needed. Chad and Skinny had kerosene stoves, but Mom cooked on the wood fired kitchen stove from Kalamazoo. Thirty-five years later, my new wife, June, and I used a kerosene stove for four years.

Mom and Pop gave their customers full service treatment. They stayed behind the counter and 'waited' on them, there was no self-service. They would be amazed if they could visit a modern Super Market with its shopping carts, rows of packaged foods, paper products and a self-service system and clerks at only Deli and checkout counters. Today, they would probably ask to each other, why didn't we think of this?

Well, the Mom and Pop groceries are long gone and buildings have been converted to other use or torn down. Those 'victims of progress' were very important citizens during the Great Depression. They provided kindness and credit to neighbors who needed their help to survive.

Supermarkets reign today and the 'milk of human kindness' has soured!

Baby Buggy to Red Wagon

Homebrew (beer) and whiskey (moonshine) were unlawful sources of income for many men during the Depression. Prohibition had banned alcohol for a few years, but homemade 'hooch' was still in demand and money could be made from making and boot-legging cheap 'spirits'. The word 'bootlegging', came from the technique of transporting alcoholic beverages illegally, by hiding bottles in your boots. The depression took away the Model A Ford but Dad and Mom owned a high-wheeled rattan baby buggy and Dad developed a sudden interest in taking my baby brother for long rides to town and around the neighborhood. My mother threw a fit when she learned he was stashing the bottles of homebrew under the buggy's mattress and making deliveries to a moonshiner's customers. They said Grandpa Hutchinson had once assisted the Sherriff locate and smash a 'moonshine still' in the hills behind his farm, but never dreamed it belonged to one of his other sons!

My grandfather Hoar, a very religious man, was visiting at the time, both would have been livid if they had learned of Dad's brief venture into bootlegging!

Mom put a stop to that fund-raising venture and traded the big buggy for a little red wagon named Dan Patch after a famous Indiana trotting horse. Kenny missed the buggy rides but really enjoyed his new transportation. Dad went out to find work every day which left Mom with three kids to manage when walking to the grocery or government surplus food distribution and Mom's answer to her transportation problems was practical. We walked like most people in the neighborhood and the red wagon doubled as a toy and means of transportation. She used it to haul Jean and Kenny and I walked beside her on errands up the sidewalk to town or a neighborhood grocery. Jean lost her ride on the way home to make room for the groceries. Money was something to be earned and the trick was to find a job because parents giving kids an allowance was unknown in our end of town.

Reggie told us the local junkyard would buy paper, rags, brass and zinc, so my buddies Chad, Tuffy and I decided to try 'junking'. Kenny had out grown the wagon, so we ran up and down alleys on Saturday mornings using Dan Patch to haul our loot. Rags and paper were easy to find but old light bulbs had brass bases and glass jar canning lids were zinc. We spent a lot of time crushing those objects to get the metal. Our goal was to find enough scrap to haul up North I Street to Rainey's Junkyard and make four bits (fifty cents) so three skinny elementary school kids could go see the Saturday matinee westerns and maybe have enough for jellybeans or popcorn on the side but by the middle of July we decided junking was interfering with our time swimmin' and fishin' time on Leatherwood Creek so we retired from the business at the age of twelve.

Saturday Trading

Saturday was the day farmers came to town to do their 'trading'. Summer and Fall were the most active seasons when they brought in eggs, chickens and garden produce to sell at the Cream Station or one of the Mom and Pop groceries. Grandpa Hutchinson liked to park his big old Dodge sedan near 15th and H Streets when the family came to town. It was a block east of the public square and the same distance west of the Cream Station. A third advantage was the restrooms, monkeys and bears at Rariden's Gas Station across the street. His children and those with families of their own and other relatives always knew where to meet for the weekly Hutchinson reunion. Dad's youngest brother, Emory, was only two years older than me and he didn't like it if I called him Uncle. We enjoyed Saturdays together as we roamed through small stores and shops around town. When shopping without money became boring, we spent time at the Gaines Blacksmith shop in the alley behind the Bedford National Bank (Chase Bank). The blacksmith always had horses to shoe on Saturday and things could get interesting when a horse decided he didn't want those iron shoes nailed to his hooves. Of course there were other interesting things to see when most of the county folks came to town to trade.

The dozens of small independent groceries in our town in those days before the supermarkets depended on farmers for fresh vegetables, eggs and other farm produce. Many had regular customers from the rural areas who did their 'trading' with them in exchange for canned or dry goods for the kitchen. In many cases, very little money changed hands. There were no credit cards in those days, but credit could be arranged with grocers who kept a record (bill) on each customer and accepted produce as payment. Our family members laughed about Grandma selling eggs at the Cream Station and keeping the money' to buy candy or 'pretties' at the Kresge or Woolworth Five and Ten stores on the south side of the square. It all evened out because everybody knew that Grandpa always brought in a few cans of cream and used some of that money for his week's supply of Brown Mule chewing tobacco.

Pipe Smokin'

One summer, near my tenth birthday, Uncle Emory and I made an interesting discovery at Duncan Hardware on the east side of the square. They sold little white clay pipes for a nickel and they were just like the ones the Leprechauns smoked in the St. Patrick's Day posters. They were supposed to be used for blowing soap bubbles, but Emory figured they would be fine for smoking. This amazing discovery came just about the time we had been thinking of trying the filthy weed. Emory said,

"Well, are we gon'na try pipe smokin' er not? I got'ta a dime for the pipes and I think we ought'ta do it."

I answered, "OK, but we haf'ta be careful, ya know we'll get'ta bad whuppin' if we git caught smoking. I thought you were gon'na make a corncob pipe."

Emory snorted," I tried making a corncob pipe, but it didn't work. Heck, we ain't likely to git a whuppin' cause we won't git caught, I've got'ta plan."

I figured he was older and wiser than me, so I took him at his word. I wanted to smoke and, after all, he had a plan that made perfect sense. There would be no smoking today, but he would keep the tobacco and pipes hidden in the corn crib until my family came out to the farm. My next question was,

"What are we gon'na smoke? I ain't puttin' any cigarette butt in my mouth!"

Emory scoffed,

"No dummy, we don't put 'em in our mouth. We strip 'em apart and put the tobaccy in the pipe to smoke it!"

He shelled out the dime to buy the pipes, hid them deep in his pocket and we started our journey around the square to 'snipe shoot' butts. (picking up cigarette butts for re-use!) Finding our supply of free tobacco was no problem. There were cigarette butts everywhere, free for the snipe shooters and we had a very fine selection. Of course, most guys smoked their coffin nails right down to their stained fingers, but a few sports flipped away fairly long cigarettes. We shot butts around the square until it was time to get back to Grandpa's car and Emory hid our supply box of butts, matches and clay pipes under the backseat of the Dodge for safe keeping until our family visited the farm for Sunday dinner the next day. Grandpa always loaded up and headed the big Dodge east around three o'clock. He claimed it was because his headlights were bad, but everyone knew he wanted to get the milking done before dark.

The next morning, Mom and Dad loaded us into the Model A for a 35 mile per hour trip out Highway 50 for Sunday dinner. Grandma's fried chicken was a big hit with everyone. We waited patiently after the big meal to sneak away when the adults were relaxing. It was a warm summer day and they were on the shady side of the porch running half way around the house. Emory gave me the high sign and we swore my little sister and brother to secrecy, before sneaking about a hundred yards out to the barn to hide behind the corn crib. It was two o'clock and the coast seemed perfectly clear for our pipe smokin' adventure. Emory got the box of butts, matches and pipes out of Grandpa's car, and we spent a few minutes stripping tobacco from the butts and packing it into our new clay pipes. Emory cautioned me to be careful with matches as he lit both pipes with one match.

We took several long puffs to join the pipe smokers of the world and filled the air with smoke as we enjoyed our new vice as gentlemen of leisure. After awhile Emory said,

"Hey, smokin's not so bad, maybe we ought'a try chawin' tobbacy next time."

He re-filled his pipe, leaned back against the corn crib to puff away and asked if I wanted another pipe full. I didn't say a word, because my stomach was feeling a queasy. I was determined to put up a bold front but the thrill was gone and I quit puffin' about the same time Emory coughed and choked trying to inhale. Suddenly, my stomach signaled that my chicken dinner was on its way up! I lost all interest in smokin' and whispered,

"Emory, I'm as sick as a dog and I think I haf 'ta puke!"

I barely managed to put down the hot pipe before I lost my wonderful Sunday dinner! I looked over to Uncle Emory for pity but he was busy holding his belly and up-chucking all over his side of our shady hide-a-way.

Smoking was giving us plenty of troubles but they doubled when two heavy shadows blotted out the sun! Dad and Grandpa had not been as interested in relaxing on the porch as we thought, or maybe they got curious about all the smoke rising from behind the corncrib. At any rate, we had been caught red-handed, there was no time to plead for mercy and none was given. The clay pipes were crushed, the tobacco tossed to the wind and the matches confiscated. We knew we had a 'whuppin' coming and they didn't disappoint us. They made us cut our own switches and gave us 'stingers' that literally made an impression on our little butts. They ushered us back to the house and everybody on the porch was smiling. Apparently, our secret scheme for pipe smoking had never really been a secret!

It was several years before I took up smoking a pipe again and by that time Uncle Emory was in the Army in France and I was in the Air Corps in Texas. We were both a long way from the corn crib, but we learned a valuable lesson that day.

Smoking can be harmful to your health!

Churches and Revivals

Religion played an important role in our lives during the Depression. Churches held many special programs to encourage attendance. Our mothers encouraged Bible School attendance and most of the gang went, because they gave prizes and served refreshments. Churches also sponsored revivals to encourage religion and save souls. Religion also came to our neighborhood with the traveling preachers and tent revivals. These were sometimes sponsored by local denominations, but more than likely they were itinerant evangelists spreading their message of 'fire and brimstone' or claims of 'faith healing'. They came to town in a car or old school bus and set up a large brown tarpaulin tent on a vacant lot for a week or more depending on attendance and money collected. The sides of the tent were rolled up for ventilation, folding chairs were provided for the audience and paper fans were often provided by the local Funeral Home. Ministers who claimed to be Faith Healers often decorated the altar platform with 'no longer needed' canes and crutches. Bystanders outside had a good view of the services and freedom of movement which I never enjoyed, because once Mom got me seated in one of their rickety folding chairs, I was there for the duration. The preaching was loud and long until they passed finally the collection plates and we could walk home in the hot summer night.

Mom liked to attend a small old Pentecost Church about eight blocks up the street which had more than its share of emotionally religious members. Many caught the 'spirit' early in the services and there was a lot of arm waving, dancing and talking in 'tongues' and the wooden floor of the old building took a beating. People in the congregation clapped their hands, stomped their feet and sang hymns. The windows and doors were open on hot summer evenings and the church services could be heard all over the neighborhood. Admittedly, some people went for the show rather than for religion. Men and boys hung in the windows or waited outside to walk wives or sweethearts home after the services. I remember one time Chad and I decided we would dress up. Our shoes were worn out so we made insoles of cardboard to cover the holes in the bottom, painted them with black enamel, and set them out to dry. That night we put on our 'new shoes' and walked to church and by the time we arrived, the paint had cracked and we were wearing stylish alligator shoes. The town churches carried out many projects to aid the poor and members contributed money, clothing and food to local agencies. Church doors were open to everyone, but Mom did not attend often because our family lacked proper clothing and she had nothing to put in the collection plate. However, she saw to it that we attended Sunday school and Bible schools in the summer. WW II put the fear of God in folks and Mom, like millions of parents, joined church when I went to war. I believe her prayers brought me safely home.

Traveling Shows

Medicine Shows, Carnivals and the Circus came to rural towns in the summer to provide a little entertainment. Our gang was excited to hear the news and we seldom missed the opening night. Medicine shows were small businessmen touring the country to make a living. Most claimed the false title of Doctor or Professor and cheated the public by selling fake salves, pills and medicines '. Our town had a small vacant lot just north of the square about the right size and they could move in and be open for business in a very short time. The Medicine Man had an assistant or two who provided music and helped with chores and sales. Once a crowd gathered, the 'snake oil' salesman became a 'barker' to peddle bottles of his wonderful tonic 'good for what ails you.' He guaranteed his miracle medicines to cure everything from warts to rheumatism for the small price of only one dollar a bottle! The 'tonic' usually contained a very high percentage of alcohol flavored by vanilla and a few herbs. When prohibition was in effect, the medicine man had a brisk business and customers bought several bottles for 'medical' purposes. The Medicine Show stayed only a day or so, then moved on down the road before customers discovered they had been swindled. The Professor's crew could pack up and move out of town even faster than they came in, especially if the police insisted it was for his own welfare. Everyone knew the true character of the Medicine Shows, but enjoyed the free entertainment!

Carnivals were a much bigger attraction with rides and tents set up in a semi-circle at the fairgrounds. They came to town in trailers and trucks and work crews of carnival workers of questionable character. There were a few jobs for local men or older boys who wanted to earn a few dollars setting up and taking down tents. The carnival often stayed a week with their bright lights and brassy music. The idea of a summer night with a lot of free entertainment brought in people from throughout the county. Sometimes it almost a family reunion when I met some of my long lost relatives like Frosty or Emory. Carnivals usually gave advance notice and guys in our gang had enough time to earn money for a few rides on the Merry-go-round or Ferriswheel. Dad told me to stay off the big rides because there was no sense wasting money on something that might kill you. It was common knowledge that the 'games of chance' were rigged, but suckers kept wasting money trying to win one of the tempting prizes. Games like the ring toss and penny pitch just looked so easy we had to try them a few times. Skinny's Dad said,

"Save your money, all them prizes are just cheap stuff made in Japan."

He was right because one guy won a watch with no 'works' inside! The sideshows were intriguing and some were available for a mere ten cents. We enjoyed the fast-talking, wise-cracking sideshow 'barkers' and their invitations to buy a ticket to see the Wonders of the World inside the tents. Chad got pretty good at imitating the barker's gibberish and we heard it often down on the crick. Doc and Tuffy insisted we go in to see the Bearded Lady. We went in got gypped and made them admit that she was wearing a fake beard. So we learned another lesson; the shows inside never match the illustrated banners out front. One year we went to a Carnival the first night it opened and shortly before the police shut it down because they had a 'mad man' in a cage, biting heads off live white mice. Skinny's Dad said those types of 'geeks' were usually depraved men needing whiskey money. That was one show I could have done without, but we had a lot of fun telling girls the gory details!

The Sultan's Harem with exotic dancing girls was especially interesting to the men and high school boys. The barker said we were too young to go in that tent, but he could have saved his voice 'cause we sure wouldn't waste our money on that show. Everybody knew the people in those traveling shows were after their money. Local police and the Sherriff were always on guard for thieves and pickpockets when those 'Carnies' were in town and sometimes they were moved on down the road before they were ready to leave.

The Greatest Show on Earth - news of a three ring circus coming to town was big and truly a' dream come true' for all the kids and adults in the county. The Circus advance men plastered telephone poles, fence posts and trees with colorful posters several weeks before for they arrived and everybody got ready for one of the biggest events of summer. Parents heard lots of begging for extra coins with promises of 'I'll be good' or 'I'll do all my chores' during the following days. We were really excited even if we didn't get the money, because a three ring circus was coming to town and we would see a free parade!

Being located at the intersection of the Monon and Milwaukee railroads made Bedford easily accessible from all directions. Every large circus traveled by train with specially constructed railroad cars designed to transport caged animals, elephants, circus wagons and personnel. Setting up a large circus was a major event and the managers hired local help and bought food their animals. The Hitchcock Fairgrounds were more than two miles from the train depots which meant each circus coming to town would put on a Grand Parade through city streets. Huge crowds lined the route to hear the shrill music of the steam calliope leading many brightly painted circus wagons with their cages of wild animals. The crazy clowns and scantily clad circus girls riding elephants or horses were followed by the horses of the Wild West riders. The long and wonderful parade was great advertising for the circus, people loved the free show and many were convinced that they had to go see the performers in the three ring shows of the Big Top.

The Wild West Show followed the three ring circus performance and of course there was an extra charge to see the Cowboys, Indians and trick riders. One of our gang's biggest thrills happened that memorable summer when the Tom Mix Circus came to town. We saw our hero riding Tony the Wonder Horse in the parade and were certain the famous movie star recognized our Straight Shooter badges, because he waved to us as he rode past! Not a one of us had the dollar admission for his Wild West show, but we went to the fairgrounds hoping to see him again. Our plan didn't work, so we decided to try sneaking in without paying. We went around behind the Big Top and the coast was clear. Tuffy led as we crawled under a canvas partition, stood up and there was our hero. Tom Mix was less than twenty feet from us! He was relaxing in a hammock before the big show and Tony was tied nearby, munching on a bale of hay. It was a thrill when the famous Western star stood up and faced us. We were still wearing our Straight Shooter Badges and hoped he might let us in free, but it was not to be, and in a very in a firm voice he said,

"You kids get out of here right now!"

I led our hasty retreat under the canvas and six blocks back to safety in Chad's backyard. Later Doc gave us his opinion.

"If ya' think about it, we all know why our badges didn't work. We broke the Tom Mix Club motto! It's the same old story, Straight Shooters always win, Lawbreakers always lose."

Clothing

The Great Depression was a time when people shared hand-me -down clothing among neighborhood families and school PTA groups had clothing exchanges where parents could trade clothing. Lucky kids with older siblings got a break, unless the older kid was too hard on shoes and clothing. Clothing was for warmth, not style and teachers watched kids needing a new wardrobe. One cold day the teacher took me to the PTA Clothing Closet in the basement and I wore a warm used coat home. Later in the third grade my shoes were worn out and Mom had cut out cardboard insoles to line the old brogans (high top shoes). School Nurse Schafer decided I needed clothes and shoes, so she took me to a private home on the other side of town and outfitted me with used clothing. The next stop was the big J.C. Penney store at 16th and I Streets where she bought new rough-out leather brogans with steel heel caps. Those used clothes and shoes that didn't leak, kept me warm all winter. During the summer of 1935, I saved five dollars to buy a blue mackinaw coat at the JC Penny store. I wore it two winters before passing it down to Kenny. That coat was especially warm, maybe because I had worked so hard for it! Home shoe repair became necessary when to we had to patch holes in our soles with cardboard or tie a string around the toe to keep a sole from flapping. Stores stocked shoe repair kits containing rubber soles, heels and glue. Someone in the neighborhood owned an iron 'shoe last' to loan to Dads who needed to repair family shoes. Dad put the shoe on the 'last' for a firm base to pry off the worn heels and tack on the new. If soles were needed, he scrapped the old leather sole and smeared on a gob of glue. (In those days, shoes were made of real leather instead of plastic.) The final step was to strike a match. Set the glue on fire and firmly press the new sole into the bright blue flame. Shoe repair was never guaranteed and lasted longest when worn less. Many a kid was embarrassed when a shoe sole came off at the wrong time or place!

Good shoes and school clothes were only brought out for special events like church, school or funerals. Men wore denim bib-overalls or work pant and.

boys wore overalls britches and were usually barefoot and shirtless on hot summer days. Alternate dress was wearing nothing but our raggedy britches, shirts often got in the way. 'Britches' is a word derived from breeches, English riding pants developed for horsemen and tight fitting below the knees to allow for riding boots. Ours were often patched on the knees or seat. Underwear was something we wore in the winter. Keeping britches up was tricky because we were a slim as sticks with no waistline and sometimes we used a rope to keep them up in place of a belt. I considered myself lucky to be the oldest boy in the family, because some of my buddies wore ill-fitting britches handed down from older brothers. Underwear was something we wore in the winter and that sometimes led to an embarrassing event, especially if a bully slipped up behind you pulled your pants down! Britches worked well for running through yard sprinklers to cool off or going swimming in the crick. We could run down over the hill beyond Mr. Hyde's pasture to our favorite swimming hole, Sycamore, for a quick dip. Of course, we were completely dry and hot again by the time we climbed back up the hill. Skinny dipping was preferred by most kids. However, swimming in my britches was not a problem, my pockets were usually empty except for a pocket knife and lucky buckeye.

Patching torn or worn boys' overalls or britches, especially the knees and seats, was routine for mother. Some used the white string grocers used to wrap packages instead of buying thread. We had one kid in our class nick-named Patches. Needles, thimbles, threads and pattern kits were popular items in dime stores and Sears Roebuck and Montgomery Ward catalogs sold new dresses for $2.98, but a dollar saved was a dollar earned! Mom's sewing machine was an important item in our house and her skill with needle and thread extended the life of our clothing. Kids in large families wore hand-me-downs from big brothers and sisters. The guys in our gang were glad we didn't have older sisters!

Girls often wore dresses feed sack dresses made on a foot pedal powered sewing machine. Feed sacks were also a great source of material for curtains, pillowcases, aprons and clothing. Smart feed companies soon discovered that fact and began printing sacks with colorful patterns of flowers, stripes. Some sacks could be bleached, but they couldn't quite erase the company's name and one of the knee-slapping Farmer's Daughter jokes of the time was:

Every time she bends over, she advertises the feed store

Chapter 4

Family Help

Grandpa Hutchinson's farm was only twelve miles east of town on Highway 50 and our family visited often. Dad helped with the farming and Mom with housework. The new Grandpa was always glad to see his oldest son's family and of course, I held the honored position of 'first son off the first son!' The farm was my favorite place to visit, because Grandma provided our family with butter, eggs and milk on each trip. It was my parents' best source of milk, meat, vegetables and other 'vittles' during the Great Depression. Grandpa Hutchinson's farm operated on man and real horse power with horse drawn equipment. Dad was the oldest of six boys, so Grandpa had plenty of farm hands. It was a complete farm with chickens, pigs, milk cows, horses and mules. My uncles, Dad's mean little brothers, often saddled Ned, their little white saddle horse to give me rides. Another of my favorite steeds was, Brownie, the old mule Grandpa hitched-up to till the corn in early summer. Mules were famous for never stepping on the tender green shoots growing in the rich soil. We made dozens of trips up and down the cornfield with me riding high on the harnessed mule and Granddad trudging behind with long reins around his neck and gnarled hands on the plow. I developed my love of riding early in life.

Farmers worked long hard hours to plant, tend and reap a harvest. Farm children quickly learned the old adage, 'A farmer works from dusk 'til dawn, but the farmer's wife is never done!' Fields were plowed and seeded by a man behind a 'walking plow' and later a planter pulled by a horse or mule. Many farmers preferred a mule when tilling fields to keep soil loose during hot summer months. Mules were more careful about stepping on the growing plants. Working the fields in summer was hard on farmers and work animals. Dad was tilling a cornfield on the Rariden farm one hot July day and the old mule died from heat exhaustion. Hauling and transportation around the farm was a wagon behind two horses with full harness. Automobiles were expensive, but Grandpa had a big old Dodge in the barn for trips into Bedford. However, like many farm famers, he hitched up a wagon or buggy for trips to the General Store, blacksmith or other business in Leesville. At one time or another, two of Granddad's brothers were teachers at the Leesville High School. Two others became college professors in the South. His fifth brother, Charles had a nice farm a mile or two down the road. Grandpa Hutchinson's farm was a very active and productive place in those days when it was operated by the old man, six sons and two daughters.

Gas Stations and the Model A

Filling stations (gas stations) were all over town before WW II and some were operated by grocery stores. The owner probably lived in the neighborhood and provided loafing benches for those who stopped by to discuss the weather and politics or maybe just whittle a while. Most stations had regular customers who ran a gas bill. The competiton was keen and drivers often benefitted from local 'gas wars'. Gas was thirteen cents a gallon and a man could drive all week for a dollar. Attendants were quick to check your oil, tire pressure and clean the windshield. We called them 'filling stations' but they preferred 'Service Station' because they offered many free services to customers. Their motto was 'Service with a smile'.

The large cold drink box with sliding tops and a bottle opener on the front was a very important piece of equipment on summer days. It was full of glass bottles of cold soda pop like RC, Coke and Nehi floating in water and chunks of ice. Kids and with a nickel were always welcome to reach in, pull out a cold bottle of pop dripping with cold water, pop off the lid and enjoy a hot summer drink I bought RC because it was the biggest bottle. If you didn't have a nickel for pop, you might swipe a piece of ice or stick your arm in for a minute to beat the heat. They paid a penny bounty for returned bottles so on days when we were broke, we scoured the neighborhood to find at least five empties to buy one cold drink. Sharing a large bottle of pop was better than nothing on a hot summer day, of course you had to control the number and size of 'swallers ' each guy took. Throw away aluminum cans and plastic bottles were years in the future. Soft drink trucks made weekly delivery and picked up cases of empty bottles to be washed and refilled! Some of the guys pounced on fruit jars and pint or larger bottles to sell to local bootleggers making beer, wine or whiskey. Moonshiners didn't need bottle caps, they had plenty of corks, but checking trash cans in the alleys was another way of picking up extra change.

Early Filling Stations used the old gravity fed pumps with the glass tanks on top. The customer would pull up to the pump in his Model A Ford, honk for service, and order a few gallons and there was a short wait while the attendant pumped the proper amount of gas into the glass top of the pump. A brass gauge on the tank indicated the number of gallons ordered. The gas tank on a Model A was directly above the dashboard and the gas gauge on the dash was connected to the tank. The attendant removed the gas tank cap, on top the hood in front of the windshield, inserted the nozzle and gravity allowed gas to flow down through the hose into the tank. The car had no fuel pump so gas fed directly from the tank to the carburetor. Other features included a cloth top, a gas throttle and spark lever on the steering column and a choke on the dash board. The gas pedal on the floor was next to the brake and clutch pedals. The driver used the 'clutch' to change gears with the 'stick' gearshift on the floor. No one dreamed of an automatic transmission. The heater was a pipe through the floor board to the hot manifold on the motor. However, the car was a great improvement over the Model T and probably the best car for the Depression. The mileage was great, the twenty-one inch wheels handled the poor roads and the dependable old 'flivver' had more steel in it than four of today's cars. Several years later, I owned three Model A Fords and June and I drove the last one on our honeymoon trip sixty–eight years ago. The little four cylinder motor would move you right on down the winding state roads (no four lane highways) and the mileage was great at thirty-five miles per hour.

Today, one minimum wage clerk manages ten or more self-service pumps, customers do all the work and millions of jobs have been replaced by computers.

Frosty's Farm

Visits to cousin Frosty's farm were exciting because he had a horse we could ride like cowboys. Aunt Gladys and Uncle Ray, lived in a nice country house on a large farm north of town and I was a ten year old city boy who loved that my entire family were farmers. Dad moved us to town when I was four, but I was fascinated by farm life and the great outdoors. Frosty, a shortened version of Forrest, was a cousin my age and I envied his life in the country. There were all kinds of things for us to do and Frosty was glad to see me. Uncle Ray didn't own the farm, but was a tenant farmer who managed it for the owner in return for free rent and a share of the profits from the farm's harvest. Our family's visit was a major event which required keen planning. Aunt Gladys wouldn't have enough cooked for company if we just dropped in and we definitely wanted one of her big meals. One time we arrived before the noon meal and didn't get an invitation to eat. We visited on the front porch and Frosty and his parents took turns slipping out to the kitchen for a bite. Of course, my pesky cousin, gave me a wink and a belly rub every time he came back to join us. I didn't mind a bit because that was his sign that he had sneaked out a bean sandwich for me when we went to the barn. Bean sandwiches were Frosty's specialty, he just cut a biscuit cut in half and slapped on a spoonful of beans, but they a real treat for an empty stomach. Of course I bragged on his idea and enjoyed a bean sandwich every visit.

After that 'no meal' fiasco, the first item on Mom's agenda for a visit was to get Aunt Gladys and Uncle Ray to invite us out for a free meal. The other option was to wait until Uncle Ray needed Dad's help on the farm. Dad was usually available for a work project because he didn't have a steady job. He was one of those twenty-five percent unemployed men in 1935. One day I heard him tell Mom,

"Any time I drive all the way out there to work for a dollar a day, my sister is going to give us free meals. Our Model A don't run on air".

The farm was ten miles out of town which was a fairly long trip in our old Model A Ford. Invitations were received by mail or in person, since neither family had a phone. Dad had to make sure the car was up to the trip and scrape up enough money for .13 cents a gallon gas. Each event was a working vacation and the five of us would pile into the car for a meal in the country.

The old car chugged bravely out the Pleasant Run gravel road with Dad behind the wheel and Mom holding my four year old brother Kenny on her lap. Seat belts were many years in the future Sister Jean and I had the entire back seat to ourselves were free to bounce all over that area or hang out the window to cool off. The farm had two entrances, but Dad chose the nearest one which was 'rustic' but a mile closer. We followed a dirt road through the woods down to a small creek with no bridge. Driving through the shallow water was no challenge for the car's nineteen inch wheels as it splashed through the water and up the hill to the house. Steep hills were not a problem to a Model A. Dad said his first car, a Model T, had no fuel pump and depended on gravity-flow to feed gas from gas tank to the carburetor and he often had to turn around and back up a steep hill. They put the Model A tank up high behind the dashboard and solved that problem

The big farmhouse sitting in the deep shade of several large maple trees was huge compared to our four room board and batten home in town. I was impressed with the large front porch and the fireplace in the living room, However, I thought the pump over the kitchen sink w as an unbelievable luxury, because they had water right there in the kitchen and we had to carry it from a neighbor's house to a dry sink. Sometimes, Uncle Ray needed Dad's help for more than one day and we stayed overnight. Sleeping space was limited during those visits and I had to sleep at the foot of the bed or a pallet on the floor. I was a sleepwalker and sometimes got up and wandered around the house. One night Frosty fixed it so we were allowed to sleep in a rickety folding bed in the spare bedroom. Late that night I did one of my sleep-walking acts in the pitch-black room and woke up trapped under that bed. Well, I had the choice of staying penned down until sun-up or waking everyone in the house. Of course, it didn't take long to make that decision. I yelled for help and drew a crowd of disgruntled sleepy people who began laughing when they saw my predicament. I'll never know how or why I crawled under that folding bed, but Frosty never let me forget it!

My favorite perk of a visit to the farm was playing cowboy and riding Frosty's horse. The farm was home to several work horses and a fat little saddle horse named Stormy who was tired and gentle enough for kids. However, there was no saddle. Uncle Ray had only a bridle and rode him bare-back when he needed to check on cows and calves scattered over the farm's pastures. Stormy was usually loafing near the big barn and we could use a bucket of feed to lure him into his stall so Frosty could slip on his bridle. Sometimes we had trouble mounting and slid off his back, but that never phased the gentle old horse. He simply looked back with an expression that seemed to say, 'Well, climb on, I can't stand here all day.' Eventually we climbed aboard and were set to ride the range, which was a fairly level pasture from the barn along the creek so our trusty steed could take a drink when needed. Riding double and bareback on the fat horse was tricky, but Frosty hung on to the reins with one hand and the long mane with the other. I hung on to Frosty, clamped my short legs around Stormy's belly and hoped for the best.

The little creek flowed over a solid rock bottom and had no swimmin' holes, but there was one spot under some willow trees where water spilled over a rock ledge into a pool about three feet deep. It was a dandy place to sit in the shade, soak in cool water up to our waist and listen to a miniature waterfall. It was a perfect spa to beat the summer heat after a ride. Riding Stormy away from the barn took a little urging, but he was agreeable to short trips. Long rides were a different matter because he had a time-limit for our rides. Like all horses, he knew oats were served in his feedbox in his stall and was much harder to control once we started back toward the barn. It was a faster ride, because visions of oats in his feed box gave the old horse more energy. Galloping across the pasture was fun, but hanging on was a battle and sometimes Stormy won, we tumbled off and he headed for the barn. Our mothers said the horse was too wild, but Uncle Ray just laughed and called it 'barn fever.' Me and Frosty had other names for it.

There was nothing to do when he dumped us, but get up, dust off and stroll down to cool off in the creek! Frosty's idea of punishment was to let Stormy go to the barn, stand in his stall and stare at his empty feed-box until we were ready to take off his bridle, then we would walk away without serving him oats. He reasoned that it might convince him to slow down on the next ride. I agreed with my cousin's strategy as we splashed around a while longer before going to the barn. Frosty had a good theory, but old Stormy never bought it.

One steamy August day we were riding along the creek toward the barn and Stormy stopped beside our pool. He had decided it was too hot for a ride about the same time we decided it was too hot to be sitting on a sweaty horse. We slid off his back, took off the bridle and let him wander off. Meanwhile, while we stripped down for a dip in the cool water of the deep hole. We assumed Stormy would roll in the dust a couple of times and go back to his stall in the barn. We turned in time to see him wander into the creek a few yards upstream, splash water with his hoof a couple of times and take a drink. Disaster struck when he raised his tail and dumped a load of manure into the water. We could only stand and watch as his entire deposit of 'horse apples' flowed slowly past and slid over the ledge into our pool. He cancelled our cooling-off plans and left us standing buck naked in ankle deep water.

We called it Stormy's Revenge

Aunt Nett

Mother's Dad and the families of her two brothers were far away in Illinois, but she had a pair of aunts and uncles living in her Indiana childhood neighborhood near Hardinsburg and Fredericksburg. She enjoyed visits to Dad's family, but three or four times a year she wanted to visit her family. Uncle Aunt Nett Mille's cabin and Clark's farm were forty miles south of Bedford and too far to visit very often during the Depression. They were Mom's only family contacts and she treasured the trips we made when Dad was able to manage transportation. We were unable to visit the Illinois area until after the war.

Aunt Nett and Uncle Clarence Miller's farm was two miles up a gravel road in the hills behind Hardinsburg, Indiana. Nett was my Grandmother Hoar's sister. She was one of the Marshall girls who married and did not migrate to Illinois with her brothers' families. She lived only a few miles down the road from her childhood home. Years later I learned that their mother, (my-Great-Grandmother) was a girl who came from England as an indentured servant to work as a housekeeper for a well-to-do Hardinsburg family. Indentured servants were called 'white slaves' and were made to work very hard, but Great-Grandmother worked until she had re-paid them for the cost of her sea voyage and married Great-Granddad Marshall when she had worked off her debt.

Nettie's log cabin was two hundred yards off the county road. The long dirt lane through the woods to their farm had several potholes for a car to navigate and when it was too muddy, we parked and walked to the cabin. The farm consisted of about forty acres, a two room log cabin, small barn and a couple of out- buildings in a clearing deep in the woods. The log cabin contained only the bare necessities and had no electricity, water or toilet facilities. We always stopped to visit a filling station's facilities and drink our fill before driving up the hill. We were not to drink from their water bucket, because they had to carry water from a spring down over a steep hill. Mom reminded us to play in the yard, stay out of the woods and watch for copperheads. We never ate a meal or took any vegetables offered by the old couple because we were just stopping by on the way to Uncle Clark's and they needed it more than we did. We kids did get inside the cabin a few times when it rained or was too cold. I remember Aunt Nett had papered the walls with newspapers so many times that it was like being in a cocoon. The corners were almost rounded from her efforts to keep out the cold. Uncle Clarence said her work added to the insulation provided by the cabin's thick logs and he enjoyed reading old news on the wall. There was a small lean-to over the rear door to store a supply of dry firewood. A small cook-stove, table and two chairs filled the kitchen and the larger room had a big stove, two chairs, a bed and a small table for the coal oil lamp. Aunt Nett had nothing modern but she coped with life each day and lived until age ninety-five.

The old couple depended on relatives or neighbors for transportation, but they were healthy and often walked the two miles to town for groceries or to earn money from odd jobs. The farm had a large garden, chickens, two milk cows and a couple of pigs to butcher for winter. Uncle Clarence had built an unusual henhouse to protect their important food supply. It was surrounded by a six foot fence made from hundreds of thin sassafras poles stuck in the ground and laced together with wire. He used longer poles to span from the fence top to the henhouse roof. When I asked him about the henhouse he laughed and said,

"Well, I have to pertec my hens from all the varmints in these woods. This way, I keep the chickins in, the foxes out and I got'ta twelve guage scattergun for any hungry chickin hawks, 'coons or weasels that come around. I tell folks, if trees wuz money, I'd be a rich man."

The old man hunted in the big trees of the hills and I'm sure he and Aunt Nett often dined on squirrel gravy and biscuits. Mom said it was no surprise that they had plenty of wild varmints for neighbors, because trees surrounded their three small fields and they lived in a forest. I was glad there were a few Buckeye trees in the yard. The two-toned brown nut looked like a deer's eye and everybody knew a buckeye brought good luck. I filled my pockets every fall to use as trading material with the guys at school. People said a buckeye helped ward off the aches and pains of rheumatism. Old timers carried a few in their pockets and swore they worked and I wasn't about to pass up that piece of medical information and I certainly needed the benefit of a good luck charm!

Uncle Clarence had a good supply of wood and kept a stack of logs and limbs in the front yard to provide fuel for the cabin stoves. His sharp axe was usually buried in the chopping block and he didn't mind if we sat on his sharpening contraption. It was a steel frame with a bicycle seat to sit and pedal to turn the large round grindstone to sharpen his axe. His double barrel shotgun, always loaded, rested on pegs over the cabin door where he could grab it in a hurry if he heard a varmint outside. Dad said Uncle Clarence was a good hunter who kept fresh meat on the table. He appreciated Dad' help with chores, but he never would let Dad help carry water up from the spring over the hill. Dad said he'd bet a dollar that the old hillbilly had a 'still' at the spring and knew more than a little bit about the local moonshine and bootleg business in those hills!

Uncle Clark's Farm

Uncle Clarkson Hoar and Aunt Alice lived on a forty acre farm near Fredericksburg, Indiana during the Depression. Early in their marriage they had 'gone west' and homesteaded in Oklahoma, but they gave up and returned to live in their home community. They raised their own food and had extra to sell or trade with the Huckster Wagon or General Store. Their only son, Emerson, died shortly after graduating from college and Clark's brother, Uncle Charlie, was the only close relative in the area. His older brother, Claude (my granddad) had moved to Illinois in search of a better life. The lonely old couple was pleased to have my mother's family come down for a visit and hearty farmhouse meal. Fredericksburg is a long way from Bedford when you are traveling in a 1930's car and since we sometimes didn't have a car, it was even farther, but Dad managed to find transportation. Sometimes he borrowed a car, other trips he promised the owner a free chicken dinner to drive us down to the farm for the day. It was a lot more fun when he was able to rent a car so we could stay overnight.

Uncle Clark liked Dad's help around the farm, was glad to visit with Mom and enjoyed having little children on the farm. He was interested in education and I can't remember a visit that he didn't ask how I was doing in school and then sternly ask,

"Well, do you think you will ever amount to anything?"

Of course I always said yes and maybe his question helped me want to do better. Mom saw the visits as a sort of 'home coming' because she had spent her childhood in that neighborhood. It was exciting to pull up in the farm driveway and be welcomed by the loud metallic cackling Guinea hens roosting in the orchard trees. The old couple didn't need a watch dog, they had a live aerial alarm system! Uncle Clark greeted us with the same message:

"Git out and come on in, you're in luck an old hen died this morning!"

We realized that of course an old hen had died. That morning he had cut off her head on the chopping block, doused her in a pot of boiling water and plucked off her feathers to prepare her for Aunt Alice's cast iron stew pot. Aunt Alice took special pride in serving up a complete Sunday chicken dinner any day of the week. She deftly performed magic on her little iron cook-stove in the cozy kitchen. Her meals were special treats for our family and bountiful feasts for a Depression family of five who sometimes went to bed hungry. She could prepare a chicken dinner fit for a king and we carried memories of every meal on our ride back to Bedford. Her kitchen was small but efficient and could be closed off from the rest of the house to keep the dining room cool or hot depending on the weather. Cooling relied on open windows and screen doors to keep the flies out. Two large maple trees kept the house shaded all afternoon. I remember Aunt Alice as a chubby little lady with a large apron who kept bustling about her small kitchen preparing all the 'fixins' to enhance her chicken dinner. She didn't relax until we were seated around the dining room table with heads bowed to 'return thanks' for the sumptuous meal she had prepared. The table was loaded with chicken, dumplings, mashed potatoes, biscuits, gravy and all the trimmings. Of course there were extras like her sweet Gerkin pickles, cold slaw and apple butter.

I don't think I ever saw Aunt Alice without an apron to protect her dress from splashes and stains. She used it many ways from wiping her brow to dusting, or a potholder for removing hot pans from the stove. Sometimes it became useful as a bag to carry kindling for her stove or vegetables from the garden. I remember that big dining-living room with a large table and six wood chairs, white plaster walls, hardwood floors and walnut wainscoting. Two rocking chairs faced the black drum heating stove in the corner of the room. Visitors could find seats on the window alcove bench or pull up a dining room chair. One window provided a view east to the chicken house another let them see north to the pump and barn area. A much used door led to the side porch with a stack of dry firewood and the pump which was only a few steps farther. A hallway led to two rooms in the front of the house, the front door and porch.

I was fascinated with the farm because Clark and Alice earned their living from the gardens, fields, animals and fowl they owned. Uncle Clark had no other job; he was a farmer and Aunt Alice was a farm wife. He let us help him with chores like gathering eggs from nests in the henhouse, but cautioned us to leave the white ceramic doorknobs he had placed in nests to fool hens and encourage them to lay more eggs. Aunt Alice said it worked and the old 'biddies' cackled proudly every time they laid an egg. The half-wild speckled Guinea hens hid their nests, often up in the trees where they roosted. A major job hazard of gathering eggs was to beware of roosters who considered us thieves, trespassing in chicken territory and stealing eggs. A mad rooster would give us the evil eye, ruffle his feathers, flap his wings and strut around us like the king of the barnyard. We were leery of his threats to attack as we retreated to the house with a basket of eggs for Aunt Alice. She agreed that we were wise to keep an eye on roosters and said there was an unwritten barnyard rule:

"Never turn your back on a feisty rooster!"

The farm had an unusual water system. A well in the side yard, just off the side porch, provided drinking and cooking water. I liked to pump the handle of that old iron pump and bring the cool clear water from deep underground into the water bucket. Uncle Clark also kept a tin dipper hanging on the handle and a water bucket in case a neighbor passing by on the gravel lane stopped for a cool drink or needed water for his horse. Aunt Alice said the mailman often stopped to fill and cool down his car radiator. There was also a cistern outside the kitchen to catch and store rainwater from gutters on the eaves of the house. Aunt Alice could pump up that 'soft water' for washing or watering the garden in the back of the house. A wood rain barrel at the corner outside the kitchen caught rainwater off the other side of the roof. Most farmers liked to have a full rain barrel or two in case of a fire.

The big white house had something most country people in those days dreamed about. There was a spring in the cellar under the house! The cool water trickled from a wall and flowed across the limestone floor into several small pools before it drained under the opposite wall. Uncle Clark had a springhouse under his house to cool milk, butter or food. Of course, the cellar also doubled as a tornado shelter.

The large pigpen was east over the hill beyond the outhouse, henhouse and apple orchard. Uncle Clark said he placed it there because the wind came from the west and they didn't need the smell. Also, he could let pigs into the orchard to feast on rotten apples on the ground. It was a strong pen constructed of split fence rails something like young Abe Lincoln built years earlier and a little farther south. The pen a field with room for dozens of pigs and a shaded pond large enough to provide drinking water and cooling mud baths for all. It was exciting to feed the pigs because they were always hungry and went wild at feeding time. Uncle Clark led us down the path with buckets of corn and slop made of garbage, milk or anything else left over from the kitchen. The pigpen exploded with running pigs, shrill squeals and grunts as dozens fought for places at the hog trough. It was every pig for himself as they scrambled for food and Uncle Clark laughed with us as we watched the feeding frenzy. He said he was glad the little pigs were making hogs of themselves! Of course he never mentioned the fact that he butchered two or three fat hogs for their winter supply of cured ham and sausage and shipped the rest to market every November. They provided his main cash income.

The small pasture behind the barn had enough grass for Big Red, the buggy horse, and his milk cows, Bossy and Daisy. Near the barn was another large pond with clear water and sunfish, frogs and snakes to try to catch on summer days. The barnyard was a great place to visit and check the back pasture to locate Big Red. Sometimes we whistled for him and he strolled up to be petted, but he came at a gallop if we lured him with an ear of corn or rattled a bucket of feed.

Overnight visits to the farm meant we got to go to the barn for feeding and milking after sunset. It was a chore I dearly enjoyed. Uncle Clark lit his coal oil lantern with a match, handed me the milk bucket and we trailed behind him as the flickering lantern guided us along the dark path through the pasture. Big Red and the cows were standing in their stalls waiting for their meals. Uncle Clark hung the lantern on a nail and its flickering glow cast weird and ghostly shadows of on the walls of the warm and cozy barn.

"The dust-covered cobwebs hanging between the rafters swayed in the night air. If memories about that old barn were dollars, surely I would be a millionaire."

From a Buddy Hendricks poem

The big animals paid close attention when Uncle Clark grabbed his pitchfork to toss down several hanks of hay from the loft. Our job was to dump a scoop of shelled corn and wheat bran into their feed boxes and wait quietly while he took the milk bucket and a short stool down into the stall beside Bossy to begin milking. I fed a few ears of corn into the corn sheller and cranked out enough grain for the morning feeding. Big Red begged for more food and I slipped him a little extra and he left when it was gone. Daisy was content to munch hay or chew her cud until it was her turn at the milk bucket. Feeding the big animals in the barn was peaceful, quiet and completely opposite of the riot at the pigpen earlier in the day. Uncle Clark let me carry the lantern when the milking was done and we trailed after him as he took the heavy bucket of warm milk straight to the spring cellar to pour into a crock sitting in the flowing water. We climbed the steps, blew out the lantern and the last chore of the day was finished.

Overnight visits in the big farm house also meant leftovers for supper, but a big sausage gravy, egg and biscuits breakfast awaited us in the momrning. We were visiting long time farmers who believed in the old proverb, 'Early to bed, early to rise makes a man healthy, wealthy and wise!' Uncle Clark said he never expected to be rich, but figured it was wise to follow that advice just in case it worked. The house did not have electricity and they began blowing out the kerosene lamps a few hours after sundown. Mom would take a lamp and lead us up a steep flight of stairs to an unheated bedroom. We three kids piled into a big bed with a thick goose down mattress and the thick colorful comforter which kept us warm as toast. She reminded us of the enamel slop jar with the lid in the corner of the room in case anyone had to go in the middle of the night. I never wanted to use it, but I wasn't about to go down those stairs and make a run to the outhouse in the middle of the night.

One favorite play area was the buggy shed on the side of the barn. A real buggy was an unusual attraction for city kids. It was fun to climb up into the four wheeled black buggy and sit on the rich black leather seat. A small boxed-in area behind the seat was the only cargo space. We could remove the buggy whip from its holder and pretend Big Red was harnessed and hitched between the shafts. We took turns driving our imaginary red horse as we trotted down an imaginary road.

Clark and Alice never owned a car, they lived in the horse and buggy days. He said they never worried about the price of gas and a bus or train was always there for long trips. Old Red and the sleek buggy with the leather top was their only means of transportation for trips down the road and over the hill to do their 'trading' at the General Store in Fredericksburg. Their small country church was even closer, only a couple of miles down a country lane and Uncle Clark said,

"It's even closer as the crow flies, just close enough to hear the church bell calling us to worship on Sunday morning and far enough away to ignore it in bad weather!"

Uncle Clark and Aunt Alice have long rested beside their son Emerson in the graveyard of that small church in Southern Indiana. Uncle Clark always said Mom was his favorite niece, of course she was his only niece.

I have always remembered their kindness. They never had much, but were always willing to provide a meal for our small hungry family visiting their farm.

Hobos and Veterans

The Great Depression, fueled by the stock market crash of 1929, resulted in a national twenty-five percent unemployment rate. Banks closed and 32,000 businesses failed by 1932. A second factor was the plight of thousands of World War I veterans who had been promised a bonus for their service but were never paid. Congress had approved a bonus in 1924, but was not payable until 1945. Angry veterans called this a 'Tombstone Bonus' because most of them would be dead before they got the money. The result was a march on Washington in May 1932, by thousands of destitute veterans, many with families. This 'Bonus Army' of an estimated 25,000 demanded Congress pay the bonus promised in 1924. They camped in shanty-towns called 'Hoovervilles', named after President Herbert Hoover. There were twenty-seven of these camps in Washington, and the largest held 15,000 inhabitants. One veteran said, "War is hell, but loafing is worse". The Bonus Army camps lasted over two months. Fearing riots, President Hoover ordered the army to evict the veterans and destroy the camps. They were literally escorted out of Washington by U.S. troops commanded by a young officer by the name of Lt. Douglas Mac Arthur. The veterans were eventually successful and Congress finally agreed with President Theodore Roosevelt who had said in 1903,

"A man who is good enough to shed his blood for his country is good enough to be given a square deal afterwards".

The government approved an average $600 bonus to be paid in 1936, eighteen years after the war. The bonus did not help our family, Dad had been too young to serve. During WW II, the American Legion originated and sponsored passage of the G.I. Bill of Rights through Congress in 1944. The bill provided tuition and stipend benefits for millions of veterans returning to civilian life. The government had learned its lesson and June, 1944 while WWII armed forces were still fighting Europe and the Pacific. Congress approved a year's unemployment payment plan and the G.I. Bill of Rights for returning servicemen. This was a stroke of genius on the part of the government. G.I. (government issue) was the term for service men in World War II.

The landmark legislation eventually enabled some 7.8 million WW II veterans to secure advanced training and/or take advantage of loan guarantees to purchase homes. I was lucky enough to benefit from both programs. Two million men roamed the country during the Depression to earn money to send home to their families. They weren't the usual tramps who traveled the country, but men from all walks of life who could not find jobs in their home communities. They became migratory workers or 'hobos' stealing rides on railroads for transportation. Riding the 'rails.' was a dangerous way to travel and hobos waited until the last minute to 'hop' a freight train as it pulled out of the rail yard or slowed down on a steep hill. They rode inside empty boxcars and carried very little baggage, only a bedroll or 'bindle' consisting of a blanket and a few needed supplies wrapped in a waterproof material. A rope tied to each end allowed them to carry it over their shoulder before they hopped a moving boxcar. Hobo 'jungles' or camps were set up along railroads near towns, often on a long grade so they could hop on or off as the train slowed down for the hill. The 'jungles' provided a camping spot where they might rest in crude shelters or abandoned buildings. They often shared a pot of 'Mulligan Stew,' which was a group soup they made when five or six hobos went into town to beg for vegetables or meat to put in the pot. We saw the migrants walking town streets looking for a job and/or chore to do in return for food or a meal. They developed secret signs or symbols to pass along information and often marked places where they received help. Old lady Smith who lived near the Milwaukee tracks gave food hand-out to many of them and bragged that she never had to chop wood, mow grass or shovel snow.

Bedford's Hobo Jungle was rumored to be in the woods east of town along the Milwaukee tracks, but we had strict orders to stay away from that area. However, the temptation was too strong and one day Chad,

Doc and I were at Otis golf course and decided to take a short detour on the way home. The tracks were less than a mile north of 16th street, so half way up the road we took off through the woods for another adventure. We were as nervous as cats in the thick trees and brush, but reached the tracks without seeing anyone. Chad wanted to search the woods a while, but Doc and I overruled that idea. We agreed that maybe this hunt wasn't such a good idea and we hurried up the tracks into town without seeking or seeing a real tramp camp. We decided to ignore the well worn path to the old stone mill and the fact that we smelled smoke along our journey a couple of times. The wisdom of our 'detour' was in doubt and, we were glad to call our trip a 'wild goose chase."

Men continued to hunt for jobs until President Franklin Roosevelt established the CCC and WPA work programs and the wanderes found jobs in their home communities. Of course, there were some men who were allergic to work and they continued the life of a tramp living on the open road. Perhaps they were born under a wandering star. Hoosier, Theodore Dreiser memorialized the hobo with a song, <u>The Wabash Cannonball.</u>

"Oh listen to the jingle,
The rumble and the roar,
As she glides along the woodlands
Through the hills and by the shores.
Hear the mighty rush of engines,
Hear the lonesome hobo's call,
We're traveling through the jungles
On the Wabash Cannonball".

WPA and CCC - Federal Jobs

The hobo and job seeking transient movement ended in when President Franklin Roosevelt established two federal jobs programs of the Civilian Conservation Corps (CCC) in 1933 and the Works Progress Administration (WPA) by executive order in 1935. In less than a year, 3.4 million men were working in their home community and building and improving city and state facilities.

The government authorized in building military ammunition plants in Southern Indiana in 1940. More than 10, 000 were hired during the construction of the sixty-five square mile Navy ammunition plant and hundreds of storage bunkers at Burns City.(later changed to Crane.) A Milwaukee Railroad 'work train' of several passenger coaches hauled workers from Bedford to Burns City. It provided free rides for more than1,000 WPA workers.

The Army smokeless powder plant in Charleston used 6,500 workers, including 1,000 WPA workers. That plant's employees were forty percent women at sewing machines, making bags to hold the powder. Charlestown workers were easily recognized by their yellow stained hands from working in the powder. Large shipments of bagged powder were sent to Crane to install in large shells, mines and bombs.

There were two obvious reasons for WPA workers to quit and find jobs at these two giant Federal projects: higher salary and workers were exempt from the draft instituted a few months earlier. The WPA and CCC were successful because they took men off the streets and railroads and provided income for families in poverty. WPA jobs paid $48.00 monthly ($1.50 per hour) and Lawrence County officials found jobs for 2,400 men. More than 250 CCC workers stationed at Spring Mill State Park planted thousands of trees in Lawrence County forestry projects. Young men in the program lived in military barracks and worked with forestry, soil erosion and civic projects. They were paid $30.00 a month and required to send $27.00 home to the family. WW II ended both programs in 1941 and most CCC men volunteered for the military.

Dad's WPA job pulled us out of a deep hole, as our family was getting bigger, appetites were growing and there was not always enough food on the table. I weighed in as a 150 pound six-footer when I was drafted at age eighteen. He earned $48.00 a month and some days I took his lunchbox to him when his crew was working in our end of town. It usually contained a couple of biscuits, a five-cent can of pork and beans, spoon and can opener.

Most jobs were manual labor and long handle shovels were the tools of the WPA and it might take thirty men all day to dig a ditch which today's heavy machinery can dig in an hour. The work was hard and men were glad to lay back and rest in the cool of the evening after building roads, digging ditches or mowing parks. Honest work beat loafing on the 'Liar's Bench' in the court house yard. Life was slow, loafing became an art and there was a running joke about how slowly WPA men worked, or rather how they avoided it, in the poem about eight guys mowing:

"Two a comin' --- Two a goin' --- Two in the outhouse, --- Two a mowin"

Many said the WPA stood for 'we piddle round' but despite those shortcomings, the WPA gave employment to those who needed a job. There was no free money and men had to work for a check. They found self-respect and were grateful for a regular monthly salary. The WPA accomplished all sorts of needed public projects, including the construction of many useful parks like Otis Park in Bedford.

Chapter 5

School Days

Bedford was a prosperous growing town in 1890 and the mid-town Central School Elementary school enrollment was growing and the city fathers dedicated two new buildings in 1899. Old Lincoln, the Southside School, was located at 20th and H Streets, on the site of the present Bedford Fire Station. Old Stalker, the Northside still stands on the corner of 8th and O Streets, but has been converted to an apartment building. Taxpayers and parents were very proud of the new eight room stone castles, built to ease enrollment at Central School which stood on the same site as the Bedford High auditorium and Junior High buildings (now the Schafer auditorium). Madden School at sixth and 'H' Streets was built in 1925 to serve children in the northeast corner of town.

Old Lincoln School stood at 19th and H' Streets Photo by author

Our gang's days at Old Lincoln School began in Miss Mork's first grade classroom in 1931 and it was a great place for poor kids during the Great Depression. Chad, Skinny, Tuffy, Doc and I were there on the first day and we soon became pals. The wide wood stairways at the front and back doors of Lincoln, and a flight to the upper floor would be our traffic pattern for the next six years. Classes marched quietly in columns of twos for recess or dismissal. There was a line for the boys and one for the girls and Miss Mork soon discovered guys in our gang had too much to talk about so we were never allowed to be together. Leading the line was an honor we never achieved so our second priority was to get a pretty girl for a partner. We seldom succeeded in that department and usually ended up with a prissy one who wouldn't talk to us. I guess that was the teacher's plan.

Classroom furniture was the same in all four elementary schools, first and second graders sat at tables, Third through six classrooms were filled with wood and iron desks bolted to boards in rows of eight seats. The inkwells in the desks weren't used, but each student had a bottle of ink to use with a penholder and steel pen point. We and we had a daily cursive writing class and learned to sign our name! The teacher's desk was in the center of the room in front of the blackboard to provide a clear view of all pupils. Good eyesight was a distinct advantage for children in the back rows. Classroom blackboards were not black, but gray slate and they collected a great deal of chalk dust every day. Housekeeping duties were considered an honor, kids volunteered to stay after school and the teacher selected two each day. We all lived nearby and it was smart to get on the good side of the teacher. Housekeepers erased the blackboards, emptied the pencil sharpener, collected the felt erasers to take outside and beat together until the chalk dust was gone. The next duty was to fill the classroom water bucket at the sink in the cloakroom and wash the blackboards and chalk tray. The pencil sharpener was easy, just a simple twist and empty the sawdust into the waste basket.

Classrooms were extremely well organized. We even had hand signals for permission to visit the restrooms in the basement if we heard 'nature's call' during class. You raised your hand for permission to be excused; it was one finger for urination and two for a more serious problem. I guess the teacher needed this knowledge to estimate how long you should be out of class. If you were on the top floor, the restrooms were down four flights of stairs and wise students needed a few extra seconds to make it in time. We joked about a fictional kid named Willy Makit. Occasionally, there was a class clown who raised three fingers. He drew a lot of giggles and completely de-railed the teachers' time-study system. Of course that joker paid a severe price for his weird sense of humor, but some days I just couldn't help it!

Fourth grade was a magical school year, we moved to the top floor with big kids, had a wonderful teacher, and knew what school was all about. However, there were a few puzzling things about our big old two story limestone building. For instance, there was a cloakroom adjacent to every classroom. The name was a mystery, who wore a cloak? Of course, there was Dracula and Zorro, but they never came around. We hung our coats in the cloak room but at dismissal we were told to get our wraps! The cloak room was also the place we left our lunch box or sack lunch, which were sometimes sampled by a hungry kid headed for the basement restrooms via the cloakroom. The teacher usually nabbed and punished the culprit, or maybe he or she was added to the free lunch list. Of course, it was another matter if they were already on the list. Then, they might have to stand in the corner, miss a recess or stay after school. I often wondered why the Principal's office was on the top floor, as far as possible from the main entrance. The answer became crystal clear years later when I became Principal of the school. Most of the discipline problems were in grade four, five or six on that top floor!

Girlfriends -- I really enjoyed elementary school, my teachers and the free lunch. Our classes were made up of two types of kids: the 'haves' and the 'have – not's. The 'haves' were those whose parents had jobs and they wore better shoes and clothing that matched. They are easy to identify in old classroom photos. Those social differences went unnoticed in the elementary grades, and we were all one big happy family. My four buddies began claiming sweethearts in the fourth grade. Chad and Doc were first to be 'twitterpated' and the rest of us soon joined the crowd. The object was to get a girlfriend for a partner and hold hands when we formed a line. However, you could spend more time with her by volunteering for after school housecleaning duty. Washing slate blackboards and dusting erasers was a lot more fun with a girl.

My fourth grade girlfriend was Susie, a cute brunette who was always neat and well dressed because her Dad had a job. My clothes were always clean but often hand –me –downs from the Lincoln PTA clothes closet. However, clothes made no difference at that age and Susie liked me too. We often walked in line, played at recess and volunteered as 'housekeepers'. She was a 'have' and lived in a nice house up by Garrison's Grocery. I often walked past it on my way to town in case she might be sitting on the front porch. My school clothes were often second-hand from the school's PTA collection. They were always clean but I lived in fear that an older kid might announce to the world that was I wearing his old clothes. I developed an 'inferiority complex' early and nurtured it by avoiding a heavy social life throughout my school days. I can testify that being poor creates a low self-image and I often felt lower than a skunk with bad breath. Of course all five of us had the same problem in grade school. Some of our playmates' mothers would not let us enter their house, but sitting on the porch was fine. We faced no discrimination at our own houses, in Hyde's woods or along Leatherwood Creek. Later, we used our caddy money to buy better clothing and climb the social ladder.

Chad and Skinny bragged about getting a kiss from their girlfriends, but I never did. Susie's family moved to another school district in 1935 when we were ten and we were not in classes again until High School in 1940 and she was dating one of my buddies. No chance for a kiss there! However, as they say patience is its own reward and miracles do happen. I am now a believer because in 2016, a few of our 1944 Bedford High class met for lunch and Susie came in from out of town. We were a long time from the fourth grade at Old Lincoln School, but after eighty-one years -- I got a 'goodbye kiss' on the cheek from Susie! She was a little late, but I sure did appreciate it!

Fire Drills --- Elementary School days were fairly calm except, once a month when the Fire Chief told the Principal to ring the fire drill bell. The fire signal was not complicated, Mrs. Small rang the loud bell three times, held it down and organized chaos broke out in every classroom. Children formed a double line at the classroom door as the teacher grabbed her grade book and moved to the head of the line. Her first sentence was usually,

"Class, we are not leaving this room until you line up and stop talking"

Sooner or later, fear of being burned alive brought complete silence. We were required to line up by height from short to tall so the teacher could see if she had all her class. Some kids thought it might be because tall kids would burn slower! When the noise died down, she led our line down to the playground and called the roll from her grade book. We stopped in the basement in bad weather. The Fire Chief timed the drill, the Principal rang her hand bell to sound the all-clear and classes marched back into the building. Fire drills were a wise decision, because the old school's wood floors and stairs were treated with oil to keep the dust down. The school was an accident waiting to happen. No one dreamed that thirty years later we would move to a new Lincoln School building and a fire station would be built where we now stood.

Children walked to school in all types of weather as few parents owned a car. Rainy or snow days we dried our coats or shoes on or around the warm steam radiators and appreciated the warmth of the classroom and a hot lunch. Those of us who trudged to school on hot days usually soaked our heads at the town pump by Mr. Otis' house. However, it was never too hot for the fifteen minute outdoor recess on the playground each morning and afternoon. The dusty playground was covered with cinders from the school's coal furnace and running and falling resulted in skinned knees and elbows. Cleaning the wound involved peroxide and picking out cinder particles. Playground games were tag, dodge-ball, kickball and horseshoes.

Depression Classroom 1934 Library of Congress

The classic movie, 'A Christmas Story' presents a good example of a Depression elementary classroom. The furniture and kids' clothing are accurate. Skinny and Doc wore imitation leather aviator caps with snap-on goggles and there was always a bully to keep us in good running condition. Strict discipline made school days easier even though we had thirty-five to forty children in a class. Quiet and orderly behavior was expected of every child, and there was swift punishment for the unbelievers and woe to any kid who whispered or made unwarranted noise. One day our third grade class was going downstairs and Skinny and I were in the back of the line. Suddenly, the teacher jerked me out of line and slapped my face for making too much noise. I explained that it was my brand new clodhopper shoes the nurse bought for me, they had built-in steel heel caps. She apologized profusely, gave me a big hug and I became 'teacher's pet'. A few weeks later, Skinny said he wished she had slapped him too!

Every teacher had a paddle and freedom to use it when poor behavior interfered with learning. Parents supported teachers and gave their children a warning which is still a very effective to encourage learning.

"If you get in trouble at school, you'll be in trouble when you get home!"

Paddling didn't hurt as much as having classmates jeering and laughing about your punishment. Notes to parents were an important means of communication in those days because few families had telephones. Children could be relied upon to get those notes home for a parent's signature. Woe be to the kid would failed to deliver and return those messages and any attempt of forgery resulted in additional punishment. Parents and teachers imposed strict discipline and children were educated in spite of large classes and poor facilities. Teachers were dedicated making sure children worked up to up their ability and could fail those who did not. We knew that fact and worked diligently to be promoted to the next grade level. Not passed on, but certified as ready to work at a higher level.

Good behavior was expected in the community and any teacher who couldn't maintain good behavior was fired. Most kids lived with both parents in those days and parents insisted on good behavior, unruly brats made the family look bad. Dads were either working or hunting for a job and mothers were home with the kids. They used the talking method with lots of threats and little action with phrases like: "Stop teasing your sister! Don't make me have to come out there! "Get down out of that tree, don't come running to me if you fall and break your leg!"

Mom's big clincher was,

"You just wait til' your Dad gets home!"

That was the threat that got <u>my</u> attention, because Dad was a man of few words and quick to deal out any punishment Mom recommended. An immediate 'hearing was held, the verdict was always 'guilty as charged' and I got a trip to the woodshed. I had trouble sitting down at supper if Dad improvised and gave a stricter punishment. Minor crimes called for a switch or 'peach tree tea' applied to bare legs and I had to go out and cut the switch off a peach tree and we had several peach trees. A really bad 'crime' called for the 'stinger,' Dad's leather razor strap, just a few whacks and it not only stung, but left a few red stripes on your behind. Whippins' were affairs to remember and they added great back-up for Mom's authority.

Schools were under the control of state and local citizens before and during World War II and teachers could discuss the Bible and Christianity. God was still welcome in our classroom and school teachers stressed Patriotism and the threats against and our freedoms.

1944 Classroom Pledge of Allegiance

School children of our Depression became our military forces and had the grit and self-discipline to defend our nation in World War II or worked in the factories to build weapons of war. Sixteen million of our generation served in the armed forces of World War II. A half million lost their lives and thousands were wounded while fighting to preserve the freedoms we enjoy today! They became the men and women of the Greatest Generation.

Schools lost ground when they lost discipline

Self Defense 1936

'OK put 'em up', was a phrase often heard around Old Lincoln School. There were fistfights and grudge fights on the playground or to and from school. Most fights started with teasing, pushing and shoving. Roughhouse play often led to a 'dare' where one kid used the toe of his shoe to draw a line in the dirt and promise his enemy a fat lip if he stepped across it. Another challenge was to place a chip on your shoulder and dare the enemy to knock it off. No red blooded schoolboy could ignore a 'dare or double dare' without being branded yellow. That was especially true with all the other kids watching but the teacher on duty usually stopped a fight before the chip hit the ground.

Bullies and fighters were watched closely by teachers and soon learned that the paddle was the penalty. Discipline was strict and parents were expected to cooperate in getting a child to behave. A kid named Ernie Jones was the terror of our 1937 sixth grade class for a few weeks. He joined our class late in the fall semester and really didn't fit in, because he was bigger and older. He slapped around a few of us on the playground, gave orders like was boss and never lost a game, because he changed the rules. A paddling didn't seem to have much effect his ways.

Mom said that his parents had dumped him off with his grandparents and left town! Ernie was a guy who needed friends. He just didn't know how to adjust to his new family and school. He was mad at the world and had decided to take it out on his classmates. Ernie was a sixth grader who had failed a grade or two and his primary goal was to get old enough to quit school. Many of his victims thought the Principal should grant that wish. We all agreed that life would be much easier without his presence. I suspect that our teacher felt the same way. Ernie had no middle name, just Ernie Jones. We called him by his first name, but we had several others for him!

We were too small to slug it out toe-to-toe with Ernie. He whipped two or three guys in playground fights and threatened the rest of us with all kinds of bodily harm if we crossed him. We were afraid of him and were careful not to make him mad. Our best strategy was to avoid him.

Chad said it was like walking on eggs, but then we discovered his weakness and decided to take action. Our common enemy was a slow runner and hated to be called names! So, we dubbed him, Dirty Foot because of his dirty old tennis shoes. We took turns at making him chase one us home every day by yelling,

"Hey Dirty Foot Jones, bet you can't catch me!"

Parents were amazed that we rushed home so quickly to do our chores, but carrying in firewood for the cook stove and filling the coal bucket sure beat the heck out of being caught and thumped by Dirty Foot. This chasing became a game that Ernie enjoyed because, as a matter of fact, he was playing with all of us and everyone was having lots of fun, he wasn't too rough with guys he captured and soon we all became friends.

Ernie's classroom behavior improved greatly after his grandparents received a few notes from our teacher and the Principal. Grandpa Jones visited school and told our teacher to use her paddle any time it was needed. He assured her that another paddling would be waiting at home. Our former enemy suddenly had lots of chores to do for his grandparents.

If a real fight developed, the other kids on the playground crowded around to enjoy the excitement until the teacher put both fighters on the 'wall' until recess was over. They had earned a trip to the Principal's office, which usually resulted in the use of the 'board of education' (paddle) and a note to the parents of the combatants. The paddling didn't hurt as much as having classmates laughing about the event and the punishments administered by their parents when they got home. Some playground fights developed into feuds or grudge fights and were planned to be continued off school grounds. Peer pressure put both boys were in a bind because each had to answer the challenge or be branded a chicken. Fight news spread quickly among the other children and it was the 'Showdown at the OK Corral' again! A grudge fight offered lots of action for cheering spectators. However, word usually reached the ears of the teacher or Principal, often by a little brother or sister, before school dismissal. Of course there was often a tattle-tale wanting to make points with the teacher. Teachers in neighborhood schools could also use punishments like staying after school or standing on the wall at recess for a few recesses. If that failed, it was another trip to the office and notes to the parents.

Some days it was worth it when both combatants had shown they were willing to get beat up to protect their macho image. Secretly, the under-dog might have been thankful the teacher and Principal were on the ball! Sometimes during a fight, the loser might threaten to call for 'back-up, but the threat of,

"I'll tell my Dad" was usually answered with,

"Oh, yeah, I betcha' my Dad can whip your Dad!"

Nothing pleased a kid more than getting his parents into the ruckus — but that plan usually back-fired

The Free Boat

It was the last week of May, 1936 and it had rained every weekend, but the weatherman finally provided a sunny Saturday morning. The rain had stopped and I looked forward to spending a day outside. I waited until Mom opened a new box of Quaker Oats to see what gift was inside. In those days each round box had a cup, saucer or glass inside. Today, antique dealers buy and sell those 'depression glass' items. It was a creamer and she found time to add it to her collection while she cooked and dished out the oatmeal. I spooned on some sugar, poured a little milk and rushed through breakfast. I was eager to see what the day offered, no use wasting rare and glorious sunshine. I stepped out the kitchen door and Skinny's shrill voice greeted me with valuable information.

"Come on, let's get down to Sycamore. I heard that Mose found a rowboat when the crick was flooded. He's got it tied up down at the swimmin' hole. Let's go down and ask him to take us for a ride! I've already told Chad, Doc, and Tuffy. They'll be along in a minute."

Mose was almost seventeen, one of the many high school dropouts in our neighborhood. He couldn't find a steady job, so he spent a lot of time hunting and fishing. Mom knew he was a sensible guy who could be trusted to use good horse sense. She said I could go, but yelled some last advice about, not standing up in a boat, as I went out the door.

The five of us headed down through Old Man Hyde's pasture and over the bluff to see the boat. We hurried down the steep path and across the lower pasture to the crick. The water was still pretty high and there was no boat in sight. About that time, the wind shifted and we picked up the faint smell of smoke coming from the direction of the 'cave' at the bottom of the bluff where we sometime camped. It wasn't really a cave, just a large dry space back under an overhanging limestone ledge projecting from the bluff. It was out of the wind and a good place to hole up when a sudden shower came up or to build a fire in chilly weather. All the guys knew about it and there was always a pile a dry wood for a campfire. There was an un-written law that whoever built a fire, had to leave a stack of wood for the next guy. Smoke and the smell of the wood fire led us back from the creek and down along the bluff to the cave. We found Mose sitting on a log by the campfire, eating his breakfast of fried eggs from a little iron skillet. It wasn't polite to ask whose henhouse those eggs came from, but we didn't hesitate to ask about the free boat and the possibility of getting a free ride.

Mose told us he found the rowboat floating loose in the creek last Thursday and rescued it before it drifted on down into White River. He had poled it back up Leatherwood until he hit shallow water above Nine Foot. He figured we could use it for fishing or boat rides in Long Hole, a three to four foot deep stretch of water running from Sycamore all the way up to the Clay Banks swimming hole. He said that area would be deep enough to float the flat bottomed rowboat all summer and even if we didn't have paddles, we could use a pole to push it around. However, there was a major problem, he didn't have the boat. It was stuck in the riffles several hundred yards down the creek. He figured it would take all of us to shove and drag it over several low gravel riffles in the creek to get it up to our neck of the woods. So, it turned out that Skinny's information was only half right and we had a lot of work to do if we wanted to enjoy a boat all summer.

Everybody agreed that a free boat was a good idea and we immediately volunteered to help drag it up to Sycamore. Summer was on the way and the idea of having a boat to pole up and down a long shaded stretch of water was exciting. We were as happy as if we had good sense, as we followed our guide through the brush and weeds down the creek bank past the Nine-Foot swimming hole. We were eager to see the wonderful boat we might use all summer if no one claimed it. Our spirits fell when we saw the big old eight foot long wooden boat stuck in the gravel of the riffles, it was a flat bottomed, blunt end Jon-boat. It wasn't what we expected and we realized the water-logged boat would be extra heavy to push over all those rocky riffles. We were many years away from the light aluminum boats fisherman use today and it was going to take a lot of muscle to get the old boat up the creek. However, the enthusiasm of youth quickly returned as Mose explained his plan. His idea was for us to wade in the cold water with shoes on and push while he pulled it over the rocky riffle into the next deep hole so he could pole it to the next riffles. Everybody might catch pneumonia, but we liked the idea of a free boat. The five of us stripped down, put our clothes in the boat and got into deeper water behind the heavy boat. Mose waded into the cold water on the other side of the riffles, grabbed the rope tied to the front and began pulling it forward. It was easier to push than we imagined and we had the 'boy power' to slide it over the rocks of the shallow riffles into the next deep hole. Mose climbed aboard and poled our prize up the creek while we cheered and followed along the bank.

We met the challenges of the rocky riffles six times and the short spring day was almost gone before our 'yacht' was safely moored at Sycamore. Everyone agreed we should postpone our Jon-boat's maiden voyage until Sunday. The sunshine disappeared as storm clouds came rolling in so we dressed and went back to the fire at the cave to thaw out and warm up a little bit before heading home.

wMose skillfully poled the heavy boat around to put it sideways against the riffles for unloading, but his two big buddies in the front got too eager. Disaster struck quickly as they jumped for dry land and fell face down in the water. Of course, the force from their feet shoved the overloaded boat back out into deep water. The rest of us panicked, stood up to abandon ship and it was the Titanic all over again!

Our heavy tub tipped forward, filled with water and sank like a rock in cold knee- deep water. Soaked to the skin, we waded out, ignored the boat and made a beeline for the cave to build a bigger fire. Our new priority was to get warm and dry our clothes. Mose threw the entire pile of wood on the fire and flames rose high but the drying –out process went slowly. Facing the fire made you too hot while your backside froze and turning around reversed the problem. We were in a jam, until the heavy spring showers came back to save us and we all ran home in a heavy rain with a perfect excuse for wet clothes. Furthermore, there was no need to mention the free rowboat at the bottom of our swimming hole. Everybody figured we could drag it out in the summer, but once again weather solved the problem. Those heavy rains lasted three days, Leatherwood flooded and the rowboat was washed back toward White River and was probably ended up in Davy Jones' Locker.

Hoosier Hooky

Air-conditioning was in the earliest stage of development in the 1930's and that stage did not include schools. Classrooms were hot and stuffy in Fall and Spring days of our school year. Raised windows did little to cool the classrooms. It was an accepted fact that when the temperature soared into the nineties, learning slowed to a slow crawl. Teachers sometimes took classes out into the shaded yard north of our school. Shade and breezes through the huge maple trees were a big improvement, but no match for a dip in the old swimming hole or holding your head under a town pump. Those hot and humid days brought on an ailment that seemed to affect boys more often than girls. The epidemic usually struck on sunny days when classrooms were too hot and confining and fields and streams were so inviting.

It was a disease called 'hooky' and it created a strong desire to escape the chains of the classroom in a flight for freedom! The antique word 'hooky' is now known as skipping school! Fifth and sixth grade boys were especially vulnerable and many caught the fever and dared to try for the impossible dream. They were well aware they faced the wrath of the Principal if caught and hauled into the office. A thin wooden paddle and a note to parents were considered the most effective cures for their affliction. Both cures were used without hesitation!

Desperate situations call for desperate actions and when playing sick at home didn't work, boys often dared to try for a day of freedom. But there was a fly in the ointment. There was a man who could track down these lawbreakers and bring them back to justice and he was the nemesis of all hooky players. He was our Truant Officer, Mr. Gruff, a very important employee of the school corporation, a necessary evil to enforce school attendance. Education was a valuable commodity and parents and school officials of the community were determined to educate every child, whether they wanted it or not. As one school board member put it:

"Teachers cain't teach 'em if they ain't in school!"

These were the days before home schooling and every kid was expected to be in a public or parochial school classroom. Any kid alone on the streets during a school day was immediately checked out as a hooky suspect by Mr. Gruff. The man was very good at his work. He knew all the hangouts and swimming holes hooky players might choose. Many 'escapees' were hauled back to justice in his big black sedan. He just never seemed to appreciate the fact that hooky players justified his job!

Kids could have eliminated his job by staying in school, but there was no danger of that in 1936.

Taking a Day Off

It was Spring and the warm muggy weather convinced me and Chad that we should g play hooky. Our sixth grade classroom had been extra hot all week and our teacher, Old Miss Mudd, she must have been 35, was getting crankier every day. Teaching was a difficult job, classes were large and salaries were about as low as teacher morale. Teachers were glad to have a job and most were dedicated to educating their pupils. Teacher tenure was hard to come by in the Depression, but there was a story told about spunky Miss Mudd.

One day at a PTA meeting a visiting school board member, who thought he knew her, said:

"Good afternoon, you look like Helen Black"

Miss Mudd just smiled and said,

"I don't look to good in brown either!

We had been planning a hooky day since the temperatures started rising in early May. We just figured we could get away with a 'day off' if we played our cards right. Chad thought Friday would be the best time to make our break!

His plan was simple, yet sure-fire. We would leave home with a sack lunch as usual, but start late and linger along the way until the other kids went on to school. It would be easy to sneak off over the hill behind the school, past the slaughter house to Leatherwood Creek. Chad's little brother, Joey, wanted to tag along, but we solved that problem by telling him we were on a secret mission and giving him a very important job. All he had to do was tell Miss Mudd we were sick at home! Joey crossed his heart, solemnly swore to keep our secret and proudly strutted off to school to carry out his special mission! The teacher later told Chad's parents that little Joey delivered the message correctly but crumbled under her interrogation and spilled the beans about our hooky plans.

We missed the other guys and the dogs, but had a great morning playing along the creek. It was great to take off our shoes, roll up our pant legs and wade in the shallow pools under the big old sycamore trees along the banks. We had more fun splashing around, catching tadpoles and skipping flat rocks across the water. Sure we got wet, but that was the reason we played hooky. We figured our clothes would dry before time to go home and Clay Banks, was waiting for us farther down the creek beyond the old Cement Plant.

The water was a little bit cool, but our clothes were drying on some brush and we had a private pool for dipping before lunch. Our first swim of the year was great at high noon, but clouds were forming and our sunny day was fading away. We decided to dress and eat before we started back up the creek.

My sack lunch was great, food always tastes better when you're on vacation, however, we didn't get to enjoy it very long. The weather changed rapidly, that lucky old sun disappeared, the wind came up and dark clouds rolled in! Mother Nature had betrayed us on our hooky day and things went from bad to worse as we hurried back up the Cement Plant road. The sudden rain came down in buckets, it was a real frog strangler and we were soaked to the bone before we reached the shelter of the old Slaughter House. No animals had been killed recently, but the equipment, blood stains and manure reminded us of past events.

Our day of freedom had become a disaster and we were wet, muddy and bedraggled. The jig was up, our well laid plan had failed and a warm dry classroom seemed liked a wonderful place. It was time to consider a new plan. We could march back to school in the rain and throw ourselves upon the mercy of the court, head for home and risk facing mad parents or stay in the dark stinky Slaughter House until school was out. Our fate was decided a short time later when Mr. Gruff's big black sedan pulled into the driveway.

The talented Truant Officer had triumphed again and we were trapped like rats, but at least we got a ride back to school. However, he made us stand because we were so wet. We ran into more bad luck at school because it was an indoor recess and our 'march to justice' was witnessed by most of our classmates. Of course, Mr. Gruff enjoyed that part as much as we hated it. He strutted down the hall like a bounty hunter bringing in his prisoners.

Our principal, Mrs. Small, was a little woman with years of experience of swinging a paddle. They said she used a short backswing and a lot of wrist action. Our trial was very brief, we were guilty and Mr. Gruff was the witness for the prosecution.

Mrs. Small asked, "Did you boys play hooky?"

We nodded our heads yes. She picked up her trusty paddle and sternly asked,

"Who wants to be first?"

I gave Chad that honor and he bravely stepped forward. He didn't even ask for a blindfold when Mrs. Small said,

"Come over here, bend over and put your hands on the seat of that chair"

She believed in quick justice and Chad took two whacks of the paddle like a trooper, but I saw a couple of tears before he turned away. Then it was my turn and I was determined not to cry. I stepped up to the chair, assumed the position, gritted my teeth and waited for the pain, it was a short wait until I got a taste of 'bam, bam and thank you Ma'am'!

Boy, that did smart and I had the tears to prove it! Mrs. Small had allowed for the fact that we were wearing wet britches. She knew our two whacks would sting like four. We had faced the paddle, but our punishment was not over, because we had to take a note home and face our parents. That meant another paddling! Then, of course, there was a lot of teasing from our classmates. We had become perfect examples of what happens to hooky players and the 'Poster Boys' for those who had met the board of education!

The next Monday morning at recess, Chad said he was working on a new plan to play hooky. I told to him count me out, I had learned my lesson in Mrs. Small's office and Dad gave me a refresher lesson at home.

Soup Lines and School Lunch

A large percentage of children came from impoverished homes and it's hard to teach hungry kids. Looking at old group pictures of my elementary classroom it's easy to pick us out by our clothing. There were very few overweight kids and obesity was not a problem in those days. There was a standard rule parents gave their children.

"If you're at somebody's house at mealtime, don'cha beg but if they ask ya' to eat, by golly you eat"!

There were always food shortages at Depression homes and we ate what was offered. Depression 'soup lines' became common as Churches other agencies and governments opened community kitchens to feed the poor. Christians 'haves' rallied to help their fellow men and 'have not' adults, children, hobos and migrants were fed through their efforts. More welfare organizations set up 'soup lines,' many were for children only. One of the most impressive monuments at the FDR Memorial In Washington, D. C. depicts men standing in a 'soup line' holding a bowl or bucket waiting patiently for a ladle of hot soup and piece of bread.

School lunches were an immediate blessing to poor families and often a child's best meal of the day. Free recess milk and the lunch programs were a treat which encouraged school attendance, because in most cases there was little to eat at home. The milk lunch program during morning recess provided nutrition for all children, especially under-privileged children who often had a meager breakfast. Those who did not qualify for free milk could buy a half pint of milk for three cents. Kids went to school for food and ate it all, there were no 'fast food' diners to dull our appetites, our 'fast foods' were rabbits and squirrels.

Tables and chairs for lunch were set up in the central basement and parent volunteers served the children. Those welcome meals consisted of a half pint of milk and a hot bowl of soup or sandwich. The kitchen was a gas stove, icebox, sink and serving counter in a small space under our giant wooden front stairs. Today's Fire Marshal would have a field day writing-up the safety violations in that kitchen which served much needed food to so many hungry children. Due to lack of space, children who brought lunchboxes or sack lunches ate at desks upstairs in a second lunch duty teacher's classroom. In 1939, Stalker School became the first school to secure federal funds for their lunch program.

The school lunch program was one of the most effective local programs of the Depression because it directly improved the health and mental attitude of children living on the edge of starvation before World War II

Bedford chool officials were very concerned about the poor health and nourishment of under-privileged children and a school doctor and nurse were hired to work with Red Cross and PTA groups. Local historian, James Guthrie reported in his book, <u>A Quarter Century of Lawrence County History:</u> "In the mid 1930's, School Doctor R. E. Wynne and Nurse Grace Shafer examined 1,267 pupils of Bedford schools and discovered; 935 with defective teeth, 817 with deceased tonsils, 369 had adenoid problems, 219 had poor vision, 503 were under-nourished and 835 lacked vaccinations. I remember lining up for those grade school examinations and my name was included in at least three of those six categories. The Red Cross and Parent Teacher Association did admirable work in the schools and its primary function in Depression years was aiding under-privileged children. In one year, the Stalker PTA (parents and teachers) paid for four tonsillectomies, four pairs of glasses, the extraction of 65 teeth, contributed $120 to the school milk lunch program and established a school library."

I had a cold in the fourth grade and School Nurse Schafer said my tonsils should come out but Dad said no. My throat got better and I missed getting a few days out of school and lots of ice cream. Doctors quarantined' families to prevent the spread of contagious diseases. Scarlet Fever and smallpox were the most dangerous but kids with mumps, measles or chickenpox were also quarantined. . Cooks and helpers were very careful to avoid contact with the sick and usually left the meals on the porch. . I remember when our family had the measles and that sinking feeling when a man tacked a blazing red 'Quarantine' sign on our front door. We were isolated worse than peasants with the black plague until Doc gave the okay to take it down. After that episode, Dad made sure we had a pile of wood and coal big enough to heat the house for a month!

Neighbors would lend a hand in the event of disease, a new baby or accident. A death in the family called for a 'wake' and people were quick to carry in food and drink for relatives and friends who came for visitation at the home or church. Some stayed to sit with the casket all night. It was a time when helping and doing the right thing was important, because they never knew when they might be in need of help. Men chopped firewood or did outside chores while women ran errands and provided meals for families confined in their homes.

"Perhaps, the true Christian spirit is most practiced in times of need, poverty or tragedy when everyone is in the same boat".

Crossing the Tracks -- Leaving Lincoln School for grades seven and eight in the old Bedford Junior High school was a real psychological jolt. We had to leave our neighborhood school and walk an additional seven blocks across town to an ancient three-story brick Junior High School. We also faced big changes of a new daily class schedule of home rooms, study halls, and changing rooms and teachers for each subject. Gone was our classroom with one teacher the entire day and we were in classes with strange kids from the other schools. The Central Elementary School, Junior High School and High School buildings were located in the same block.

Chapter 6

Buggy Ride to Uncle Billy's

Fall Saturdays were special to teenagers who had spent the week penned up in a classroom after a long summer vacation. Winter wasn't too far away and fair weather deserved to be spent wisely. This Saturday morning, me and Chad had an okay from our parents to hike down the road to visit Chad's Uncle Billy and Aunt Mary. They lived on a small farm about four miles south of town and Uncle Billy had often invited us to come out for a visit and this was the day. The old man didn't get around too well anymore and he was always glad to have company, especially if they were willing to listen to his stories about the old days. Uncle Billy didn't own a car, he traveled by horse and buggy and when he came to town, he usually tied his horse, Dolly, to the 'hitchin' rack' at Grubb's grocery at 24th and I Streets on the south edge of town. He didn't like driving in town traffic so he hobbled six blocks up to the town square if he needed medicine, hardware or something the grocery didn't stock.

We were free, it was a crisp fall day and the leaves were beginning to color. Our first stop was Grubb's grocery store to check the hitching post. Weekends, we kept an eye on it in case Uncle Billy and his old horse came to town. Sure enough this Saturday, Uncle Billy's transportation was tied to the hitching rack. We seldom missed a chance to pat his grey mare, Dolly. It was fun to feed her wisps of grass or clover while she patiently waited to make the trip back home.

Uncle Billy came back from his errands and was glad to hear we could enjoy a buggy ride out to the farm. There was very little traffic in those Depression days. People who did own cars could not afford to drive them as gas was thirteen cents a gallon. He said our dogs wouldn't be a problem and they could ride, except going up hills. I knew my dog, Collie would behave but I wasn't too sure about Chad's new dog, Bingo. We found a seat in the rickety buggy and Dolly was soon trotting down South I street with a load of three people, two dogs and three sacks of groceries. The dogs seemed to enjoy the ride while Chad and I took turns perched up in the bouncy driver's seat beside Uncle Billy. Dolly slowed to a walk when we reached the steep I street hill down to the Leatherwood Creek Bottoms. She walked carefully down the side of the road to keep her iron horse shoes from sliding on the hard surface of the blacktop road.

The fall morning was heating up by the time we reached the bottom of the hill and Uncle Billy pulled off the road to go down the shady lane to Nine Foot, a popular Leatherwood Creek swimming hole. Dolly was familiar with the routine and headed for the shallow riffles of water flowing from our swimming hole. Uncle Billy drove his horse and buggy directly into the shallow water of the creek for a cool drink. The clear water rushing over gravel riffles was a strong temptation on such a warm day. Both dogs had already bailed out into the creek and me and Chad could think of no reason not to join them. We stripped down and hit the water about the same time. Dolly ignored all the commotion as we splashed in the cool water until we were soaking wet. We were puzzled when Uncle Billy pulled the reins to guide Dolly and the buggy back into trees on the shady bank. He explained that you should never let the hot horse drink too much or she might 'founder' and ruin her hooves. So, the scene changed quickly, Dolly was taking a breather tied to a tree while Uncle Billy was taking off his boots! Next thing we knew, the old man was wading and splashing in the riffles with us! He waded in to deeper water to join us in vigorous water fight. I guess old men seldom foundered!

We ended our rest break, dressed, climbed back into the buggy and Dolly trotted out of the shade back to the hot blacktop road. Collie and

Bingo curled up in the back to snooze and dry off. Once we were on level ground again, our chauffer asked if we would like to take turns with the reins during our journey across the bottoms and Leatherwood bridge. We both wanted to be first, but Uncle Billy said it would be fair to draw straws. I was a happy kid when I showed Chad the long straw and climbed up front to take the long leather reins to drive our 'chariot' until we crossed the bridge where Chad took over until we came to the base of the steep hill going past Bright's Dairy farm. Uncle Billy took the reins for the climb and explained that we needed to lighten the load, but promised we could ride and drive again when we reached the top. Chad, me and the dogs jumped out to walk up the hill behind the buggy.

Walking up the hill was peaceful and quiet until Collie and Bingo saw the cows and went nuts and barked like mad when they saw dozens of huge black and white Holstein cattle lying in the shade on the hillside across the fence. Perhaps their egos where shattered when the cows ignored them Walking up the hill behind the buggy to help Dolly was quiet and good exercise and calmly chewed their cuds. The entire dairy herd paid absolutely no attention to the frantic dogs as our noisy little caravan moved slowly up Bright's Hill.

We mastered the hill and everyone piled back into the buggy because the road ahead, a section of the Poor Farm Road, was as flat as a tabletop and the last leg of our journey. Uncle Billy started telling stories and Dolly didn't really need steering, but we kept a tight grip on the reins as we took turns riding the front seat beside Uncle Billy. Our instructions were to let her walk across the flats. Both dogs were curled up in the back and very quiet, maybe hoarse, as we moved along. Actually, there was very little driving because the old horse probably knew the way home blindfolded, but holding the reins of a fast moving horse was a real treat. The mare seemed a little winded, but she trotted a lot faster as we neared the farm. Uncle Billy warned us to keep a tight grip on the reins and holding the reins of a trotting horse was a real treat, but I was sure glad Chad was driving when we pulled into the drive and the old mare ran up to the gate. Uncle Billy quickly grabbed the reins and said,

"That's okay Chad, Dolly's just acting up a little, just excited about getting home. Reckon she has 'barn fever', but she'll be cured as soon as she gets her oats and hay."

I jumped out to open the gate and Uncle Billy steered the eager mare to the barn. We watched him unhitch the horse from the buggy shafts and take off the harness. He chased the dogs out of the water trough and let Dolly have a short swig before she went into her stall. The mare had done a day's work and was ready for her vittles, but Uncle Billy turned her into a side pasture. He said she couldn't have water or food until she cooled down. We followed him back toward the house, but stopped a while to watch the little mare trot out to a dusty area in the pasture and paw the dust a few times. Uncle Billy said,

"Now, she's gotta' take a dust bath to dry off the sweat. They say a horse is worth a hundred dollars every time it rolls over, let's see how much Dolly's worth".

We called the dogs and held them while we watched as the little horse circle the dust before she knelt gingerly down on her front knees, laid over on her shoulder and her rump hit the ground with a thud. She rolled over twice and stood up spraddle-legged to shake off the dust like a dog shakes water before trotting back to her stall for shade.

Uncle Billy yelled, "Hey, I've got a two hundred dollar horse"!

Aunt Mary was sitting in her rocker on the front porch, sipping a glass of iced tea and enjoying the afternoon when we came up from the barn. She fixed a quick sandwich and iced tea lunch and threw a couple of biscuits to Collie and Bingo. We visited a while on the front porch until it was time to go back to the barn to feed Dolly. She was out in the pasture but saw us heading her way and forgot she was tired as she broke unto a gallop to beat us to her stall. She was eager for her ration of ground corn and oats. We gave the little grey mare a final pat, called the dogs and were ready for our hike back to town.

Uncle Billy said we could avoid walking the hot road and stay in the shade by taking a short-cut down the old railroad bed past his farm. He said the tracks had been taken up years ago, but the trail would lead us through a tunnel and on to the deserted Cement Plant east of town. We thanked him for the buggy ride, called the dogs out of the shade and hiked into the trees down the railroad bed toward the old tunnel. We knew all about the Cement Plant but the idea of going through a tunnel was a definite plus!

The dogs had a ball chasing squirrels and eventually caught one on the ground. That victory made their day and improved their morale which had been badly damaged by the 'Holstein cow incident'. Uncle Billy had said it wasn't a very long tunnel and when you went in about twenty feet, you would be able to see the light at the other end. However, we had our doubts as we stood alone in the shady woods before a gaping black hole in the hill. Bats flying out of the tunnel or the hoot of an owl would have sent us running back to Uncle Billy's, but the day was too far gone to turn back. About that time, Collie and Bingo came out of the tunnel as if to shame us, so we stepped into the darkness and groped the walls for several feet until they curved slightly and as the saying goes, 'we saw the light at the end of the tunnel.'

Shortly after the tunnel experience, we left the trail behind Rariden's Dairy to follow a wagon road past the old deserted house on the old Mullins farm and were familiar territory. We took time to see if the persimmon and walnut trees were loaded then followed the farm road down the hill to the blacktop road at the Leatherwood Bridge. Of course, we took time to hang over the railing, spit in the creek and watch the sunfish come up to get it. We had used up most of our day, but took time for a quick dip at Nine Foot before climbing the 'I' street hill. October weekends were special in Southern Indiana, and our trip to Uncle Billy's proved to be our last chance to enjoy a warm day, sunny blue skies and rolling hills painted by colorful leaves. I got home late and my great day ended with a scolding. Dad said,

"Why did you stay out there all day? You had us worried, you're late and by dang you can just go without supper!" My sister and brother enjoyed the ruckus and Mom continued the scolding as she followed me out of the room, but in the kitchen, she whispered,

"You'll find your plate of beans and cornbread in the warming oven and some buttermilk in the icebox."

Dad pretended he didn't know what was going on and kept listening to his radio program. He had learned that it is sometimes better to ignore minor things that were better unknown. I was in the doghouse for a week and he gave me a few extra chores but I considered my punishment a small price to pay for the adventures of the trip! Chad said he got the same reception at his house..

Hoosier weather prevailed and it was cooler and rainy most of the following week. Jack Frost's painted leaves were sailing in the wind and snow was on the way!

Thin Ice

Summer days on Leatherwood Creek were spent fishing, and skinny dipping in the cool water of deep holes like Nine Foot, Sycamore or Clay Banks, but we also enjoyed it in the winter. There were long stretches of shallow water for ice skating. Long Hole was just up the creek from Sycamore, our favorite swimming hole, and Sowbelly was just over Slaughterhouse Hill above the arched bridge.

Both were only knee deep, easy to wade into and favorite swimming and wading spot for families with small children. Older kids couldn't swim without skinning their knees on the sand and gravel bottom but they made great ice rinks. Shallow water was the first to freeze and you could always wade out if you fell through the ice! It seems that we had longer spells of cold weather when I was a kid in the 1930's. The creek would freeze for weeks at a time and the ice stayed strong enough for us to ice skate and play hockey. I use the word skating loosely because many of us slid across the ice in our shoes. However, a few of the guys had old fashioned skates to clamp on their shoes with a skate key like roller skates. One lucky day in August, I bought a pair of rusty skates at the junk yard. It was tough to keep them fastened on my shoes and not unusual for a skate to come off at a critical time in a hockey game. Ice is as hard as concrete and there were several days I limped home after an afternoon of rough and tumble games.

There was very little store-bought equipment in our hockey games. Every kid wished for a pair of shoe skates, but they were just something we hoped Santa might leave under the Christmas tree. Finding a hockey stick was easy, we just cut a limb from a tree. The trick was to find a curved limb and cut it to fit. The hockey puck could be a small chunk of wood or we could saw off the end of a stick of stove wood about the diameter of a real one. Snow never stopped our gang, we brought brooms, swept off the ice and cleared paths for hockey or racing. A big campfire on the bank and a few logs around it for seats made ice skating at Sowbelly lots of fun for Dutchtown kids in the Depression.

Thin ice or sudden thaws were two things that could de-rail any early winter ice skating plans. I remember one Saturday in 1936, when the cold winds of mid November set us to thinking the creek might be frozen enough for skating. Sometimes, we got too eager to test the ice and someone got soaked, so we developed a simple system with the dog test. Chad, Chubby and I usually had our dogs tagging along with us when we went to the creek. The three big hungry dogs were Collie, Rover and Chubby's dog, Brutus, who was especially heavy. We knew the weight of the dogs would give the ice a good test. Chad brought along a few stale biscuits for bait to lure them out on the ice. We lined up on the creek bank and new ice looked fairly strong, so we decided we should test it. Chad called the dogs, gave them each a piece of biscuit and threw the rest out across the ice. Brutus led the charge with the others close behind. Three large dogs slipping and sliding across the ice scrambling after the biscuits was a sight. They gobbled all the biscuits and returned to the shore safe and dry. Our first test was a 'howling success.

The second test called for one of us to go out on the ice. As usual, we drew straws to see who had to risk being dunked on that cold November day. Chubby, one of the few fat kids in our neighborhood, (his Dad had a steady job!) drew the short straw. He announced that he would do the job right and amended our test to include the weight of his big dog, Brutus.

"I'll go out on the ice and call him to me," he said.

We all agreed that he had a great idea, because Brutus was a heavy dog with perhaps a dash of Great Dane somewhere in his family tree. Chubby instantly earned our respect with his new and daring plan to test the ice! Skinny donated a cold biscuit to lure Brutus and we cheered the fat kid as he carefully edged out to the middle of the frozen creek, turned and held out the biscuit to tempt his big dog. Loyal Brutus launched himself onto the ice and slipped and slid to his master in the middle of the crick. For one brief moment the 'second test' was a great success and we cheered again. However, Chubby padded his role by jumping up and down to celebrate the victory and we all heard the ice crack. We yelled to warn our buddy to run, but it was too late. He and the big dog scrambled back across the ice in a mad dash for the bank. Brutus made it but the ice gave way just before our valiant volunteer reached dry land and he sank up to his waist icy water. Needless to say, he was soaked to the skin by the time Chad pulled him onto the bank..

Our gang was in trouble because we hadn't built a fire and we were a long way from heat. There was only one thing to do; get our freezing pal to a warm house and dry out his clothing. My house was closest and I figured Mom would agree to help us, because Chubby's house was two blocks farther down the street and his parents weren't home. We hurried our shivering buddy up the bluff to get him to a seat by a stove. His teeth were chattering and he was as cold as an icicle by the time we reached my house. All five of us rushed Chubby into the house and Brutus followed.

Mom grasped the situation and before you could say Jack Robinson she had Chubby wrapped in a blanket in a chair close to the pot-bellied stove in our living room and his soaked clothes were hanging on a clothesline behind the kitchen stove. We enjoyed the warm house and were happy to see our wet pal drying out by the blazing fire. Brutus was right with him, maybe he felt guilty for being dry. Nobody wanted to argue with the big dog as he lay curled up behind Chubby's chair.

Our first ice skating event of the year had ending badly, but we knew colder weather was coming to Southern Indiana and there would be more time for ice skating. There was no telling who would draw the short straw next time, but we all agreed that Chubby and Brutus were certified members of our gang. However, the poor guy confessed that he had another pressing problem, his parents had told him not to go to the creek. As soon as his clothes dried, he dressed and hurried up the street and made it before they came home. However, the poor guy's cold caused him to miss three days of school, spend his Thanksgiving vacation in bed and be grounded for a couple of weekends.

We never found out how his parents learned about his dunking in Leatherwood Creek, but I'll bet my Mother knew!

WINTERS LONG AGO

Winters were long and cold for many families in 1934. Our nation was in the middle of the Great Depression and millions of families needed help. We were definitely one of those families. Our little board and batten house on South H street was heated by a wood stove in the kitchen and a big potbellied stove in the living room. The un-insulated house was hard to heat and Dad kept both stoves hot all winter. The stoves burned coal or wood but coal was needed when it was really cold because it gave off much more heat. Our kitchen and living room were the warmest rooms in the house and a seat near a stove was the most comfortable spot in the house when Old Man Winter came around. Fuel to keep the home fires burning was a serious problem. Some men became so desperate they would hop a train hauling coal when it slowed down on the long climb up from White River trestle and throw off lumps of coal when it got closer to our neighborhood and men were waiing to carry it home in a burlap sacks. Dad cut wood on Grandpa Hutchinson's farm in the fall and stacked it in the woodshed, but he had to buy or beg for coal. Five dollars would buy quite a bit, if you had the five dollars. Sometimes, he was forced to apply for help from the Township Trustee. His major goal to have enough fuel stored in our garage on the alley to keep fires in Mom's cook-stove and the pot-belly stove through the winter. By the age of nine, I was promoted to the position of 'Keeper of the Flame' and one of my after school chores was to carry in enough wood and coal to fill the kitchen wood box and coal bucket next to the stove in the living room. It was a long walk with an armload of wood or a bucket of coal, but Dad said it would build muscles. My responsibilities also included cleaning the stoves, but getting rid of the ashes was easier, I spread those over the garden for fertilizer. The family gathered around the Warm Morning pot-belly coal stove in the front room or Mom's kitchen wood stove in the winter months. There were only four rooms to heat. The front room was our living and family room, but in the winter, it was our 'warm room' where we did homework by the light of a kerosene lamp on the stand table. Some nights the cast iron 'belly' of the stove glowed bright red radiating warmth into the room. That hot stove had to be several feet from the wall to avoid a fire and that gave us room for a couple of chairs behind it. They were especially cozy seats, because we also benefited from heat radiating down from the long stovepipe overhead.

The house was hard to heat when winter winds blew and so drafty that some nights the flame of our kerosene lamps flickered. Dad stuffed rags around the doors and windows on extremely cold nights. Our bedroom was cold and crowded. Mom heated up her sad Irons, wrapped them in towels and slid them under the sheets to warm the bed. We eagerly crawled in under a pile of blankets and comforters fortified by coats and towels. I remember feeling very snug and warm while listening to the wind whistling around our little house. Family pets often curled up on the bed, but we didn't care and welcomed the added warmth. Some said you could judge how cold it was by the number of dogs sleeping on your bed. Hence the expression, 'It was a three dog night.'

Our situation wasn't quite as bad as Bob Hope's story about growing up poor in England with his six brothers. Bob said,

"We used to sleep four in a bed, and when it got too cold, Mom threw on another brother."

We used one bedroom to store un-needed items and baskets of apples, pears turnips, yams and potatoes. Of course the important shelves were loaded with Mom's jars of canned food from the summer garden. We were in big trouble if they froze. Dad got up early to stoke up the fires in the kitchen stove and the potbellied stove in the front room. Mom got up to fix breakfast and sometimes had to break the ice on the water bucket. We kids got to stay under the covers a little while longer, warmed by our own body heat. The aroma of biscuits and gravy, oatmeal or sometimes, bacon and eggs told us when it was time to rise and shine. Food was scarce and it was not wise to be late for a meal. There was an old saying, 'That good smell from the kitchen won't fill your belly.'

My sister, brother and I warmed up and dressed behind the stove before breakfast. We wore the warmest sweaters caps, gloves and coats we owned on the chilly walk to school and never tarried along the way. Actually, none of us had proper clothing or shoes for the five block hike in freezing weather.

Black coal smoke rising from the chimney of the big limestone school beckoned us up H Street to classrooms warmed by steaming radiators. The monster coal furnace in the basement was preparing a warm and cozy place to spend the day. The thought of a half-pint of free milk at recess and a free hot lunch offered more reasons to hurry. Old Lincoln School was not only a place to learn, it was a great place to spend cold winter days with teachers that cared about us.

Snow seldom closed the Bedford schools. We had four elementary schools, one for each section of town. The Junior and High schools were centrally located. There were no school buses. Town kids walked to school in rain, snow or sunshine. Three or four inches of snow were hard to navigate without boots or high- top shoes, especially if you had hole in your sole! Sidewalks were seldom shoveled off so we walked in the street. There was very little traffic, and walking in tire tracks made life easier. Our future was dim in the poverty of the Great Depression.

The old adage, pull yourself up by your bootstraps, didn't make sense when you didn't have boots.

Bedford Christmas 1935

Stores stayed open several nights before Christmas and windows were decorated with displays of clothing, toys and gifts. Courthouse lights lit up the two story limestone building as the center-piece of the square. Winter weather determined the size of the crowd but we usually had good luck in that department. Parking spaces around the town square were full and family cars served as home base for family members who liked to watch the parade and kids who roamed the stores. Families without cars walked to town for the lights. We were in that category and Mom loaded the little red wagon for a wintry stroll up 'H' Street to join the celebration. We enjoyed lights glowing on trees in homes (with electricity) along the way and the Christmas lighting and store window displays around the town square were fantastic Mom liked the Christmas music of the Salvation Army Brass Band which played each evening on the southeast corner of the square in front of the JC Penny store. The charitable organization's building was an old brown house a short walk east of the square on 16th street, just past Fred Otis' Bedford Daily Mail. Then as today, the Army was helping the needy with much needed aid every day of the year and those with little money tossed coins into the kettle to help those with even less.

Crowds strolled sidewalks to enjoy the evening, meet old friends and share the Christmas Season. Many could only window-shop, but others filled the stores hoping to find inexpensive gifts to hide under their tree. The Fair Store and others had a live Santa in their toy department and the SS Kresge Five and Ten, Woolworth, Bill's Auto, JC Penny and the rest stocked larger than usual toy and gift selections. School children roamed the aisles clutching nickels and dimes in their mittens while shopping for just the right gift for the classmate whose name they had drawn for the school Christmas party. Our favorite Toyland was upstairs at the Fair Store on the north side of the square. The family-owned business created a toy department only at Christmas and really enjoyed watching the children parade through the store and up the winding stairs to 'window shop'. They knew most of us didn't have an extra dime to our name, but they appreciated the ten cent gift exchange money. The Fair Store went out of business years ago, but not before I bought my wife June a set of Rogers silverware for our first anniversary in 1949!

Each schoolroom had a Christmas party with a cedar tree and gift exchange. The class drew names two weeks before Christmas vacation to give kids time to get presents The price of the gift was limited to ten cents so all could participate and Teachers in grades one to six usually kept a list of the results to prevent kids trading for the name of their buddy or a particular girl. Ten cents was the gift limit, but sometimes large families couldn't afford that and the gifts were home-made. Wise teachers wrapped a few extra packages to be sure every kid went home with a gift and dry eyes. Gift exchange at school was limited to a ten cent gift, but a dime bought a lot of happiness in those days. There was no doubt about it, the Christmas treats plus a gift exchange party was the major event of the year.

Teachers and the PTA mothers provided funds for a sack of hard candy, chocolate drops and peppermint sticks. Extra treats included an apple and orange to make it a healthy treat. Some said there wasn't a lot of learning on Party Day, but there really was, because those were the days before teachers had not yet been banned from telling children the real 'reason for the season'.

Neighborhood churches distributed treats of candy at special parties and Sunday school. My buddies and I became more religious and attended as many church events as possible between Thanksgiving and Christmas. I'm sure church leaders scheduled parties on different days to insure helping as many needy children as possible could attend. Local civic groups issued invitations to special parties for needy kids identified by teachers.

We understood why we celebrated Christmas and wished each other Merry Christmas not Happy Holidays!

Little House Christmas 1934

Believe it or not, in spite of a shortage of money, Christmas was a happy time at our house. We cut a cedar tree in Glover's field behind our house and decorated it with fragile glass ornaments, aluminum icicles, strings of popcorn and colored paper chains made in art class at school. Dad ordered five or six sacks of peanuts in the shell and various kinds of candy from King's grocery.

Soft and chocolate candies were favorites and we rationed those, but they were soon history. There was a lot of hard colorful candy, peppermint candy canes and horehound sticks. We always had room for popcorn and sometimes I got the job of head popper. We didn't have to pop it in a pot on the stove. Dad had traded for a popper with a wire basket on a long metal handle. I put in a handful of popcorn, opened the stove door and held it over the hot embers like roasting wieners and it popped until done. We considered it one of the greatest inventions of the time.

Christmas Eve with gathered in the living room for Dad's 'ritual of the coconut' almost a family tradition involving one of nature's hard three-eyed palm tree products, a glass, nail and hammer. There was mild violence as he punched out the eyes, drained the 'milk' and gave us a sip from the glass before the main event. We watched in anticipation as he held the coconut in one hand and bashed it with the hammer to crack it open.

The fresh white coconut was Dad's special Christmas treat which was so different from the sweet hard candy, jelly candy, chocolate drops and peppermint sticks. Mom's favorites were roasted peanuts, so Christmas Eve we gathered around the stove for a rare treat to be enjoyed as a family activity of eating fresh coconut, munching peanuts and tossing coconut and peanut shells into the coal bucket.

Christmas day Mom cooked a big boiling hen with dumplings, sweet potatoes, opened a few jars of canned vegetables and fruit for our feast. There was never a turkey, but a big fat hen is a great substitute. Presents were simple and few, mainly a toy or two and clothing wrapped in brown paper leftover from grocery purchases. In our day, it wasn't the thought that counted --- it was the gift!

Santa Claus

Letters to Santa were great writing and spelling lessons in those long ago days. Everybody in the gang agreed that Santa couldn't bring you what wanted if he couldn't read your letter. Those letters were some our best writing of the year and probably should have been turned in for grading. We all celebrated the birth of Jesus, but we also wanted to believe in Santa Claus, the guy who brought the gifts and instant gratification!

Sears Roebuck or Montgomery Ward catalogs were very important to us during the Depression, because they illustrated and informed us of all the available merchandise we couldn't afford. We called them Wish Books and played a game we called 'If I had the Money'. We made long make-believe shopping lists for all the things we would buy if we had the money. We listed our 'purchases' in priority in case we didn't have enough imaginary money! It was a great way to pass long winter days as we huddled around the stove and waited for warm days when we could romp and play outside. I know we learned a great deal about the value of money and saving for a rainy day during those days in the Great Depression when we grew up doing without.

When you're poor, no matter what you want --- you can't afford it!

My 'wish list' was long and my 'If I had the Money' list was valuable resource material. Postage stamps were never a problem because we could mail our letters at downtown stores in special North Pole mail boxes for express delivery to Santa's Workshop! My idea of Santa's workshop was much the same as the one created in Tim Allen's movie, 'The Santa Clause'. I imagined a busy place with happy elves making jillions of toys for Santa's midnight ride. I considered Santa my best bet for getting toys because Mom and Dad sure didn't have the money to buy them! I think my dozens of letters to Santa may have honed my writing skills as I asked for the moon in hopes of getting part of my list. By 1932, at the age of seven, I gave up and reached the conclusion that either Santa didn't exist or my letters weren't making it to the North Pole, so I gave up. It wasn't too hard to let him go because he had never come through with any of the great gifts I requested. Actually, I was lucky to find gifts of clothing and maybe a couple of toys under the tree.

One year I got several items of clothing, but my only toys were three WW I iron soldiers about three inches tall. They were very durable and I have two of those rusty Doughboy veterans tucked away among my antiques.

Many of the scenes in the classic film, 'A Christmas Story,' remind me of my boyhood, although Ralphy lived in Gary a few years later. The alley fights and classroom scenes brought back many memories of my boyhood in the old Lincoln school at 20th and 'H' Streets. I too had trouble with bullies, wore an aviator cap with goggles and craved one of those Red Ryder BB guns named after a comic strip cowboy and hero in Saturday matinees. Later, I traded my roller skates to an older kid for his Daisy BB gun. Chad got a new one but we kept our 'bean flippers' handy; pebbles were so much cheaper than BB ammunition. The bean flipper was our side-arm, a homemade slingshot, which was very effective and easily fit in a guy's hip pocket so we 'carried' in are free time. Making the economical weapon was fairly easy. We cut a forked limb from tree to get a branch like a 'Y' and tied a strip of rubber from an old tire inner-tube on the top of each fork. The next step was to find a piece of leather to attach to each strip of rubber and make a pouch to hold the ammo, usually a bean or rock. The 'flipper' let you do a lot of target shooting. Kids didn't feel dressed unless they had a few pebbles and a bean flipper in their hip pocket for shooting at homemade targets, bottles and frogs as we roamed the banks of Leatherwood Creek

We were charter members of the BFA --- (Bean Flipper Association)

Chapter 7

● ● ● ● ● ● ● ● ● ● ● ● ● ●

Dutchtown Home # 2

Dad got a job with the WPA (Works Progress Administration) in the summer of 1936 and was earning $48 a month. FDR's workfare program came at just the right time. Our family of five was outgrowing the little 'board and batten' house on South H Street, so he rented a house on the northeast corner of 18th and E Streets in the heart of Dutchtown. It was a well built house, one of the many fine houses built by German families who originally settled in the neighborhood. There was even a German Methodist church, a small building with a tall steeple and a long bell rope in the entryway. I attended Sunday school there for several years and sometimes got to swing on the rope to ring that Church bell.

I dreaded having to leave Chad and the gang on south H street, but it was only a few block, I didn't have to leave Lincoln School for another year and we were still on the edge of town, near Leatherwood Creek. Mom explained the move in practical language; you will just be going to school from a different direction and we are so lucky to find a bigger house and garden. Actually she was tickled pink to have a better home a few blocks nearer the square. We now had a house with electricity and she could say goodbye to the coal oil lamps. My sister Jean and little brother Kenny would no longer have the chore of trimming the lamp wicks. An added bonus was a radio and lighted tree at Christmas. Every light in the house hung from the ceiling in the middle of the room. We needed only six light bulbs for the entire house. The kitchen light was directly over the table and was great for Jean, Kenny and I to do homework. That fact alone probably saved our eyesight for several years. We still had a house without plumbing and a two-hole outhouse down on the alley, securely nailed to a barn. Our water supply came from a town pump just across the street on the northwest corner of 18th and E streets! It was about the same distance as the faucet in Auggy's basement.

Moving to a bigger house greatly improved the quality of life for our family; we had moved uptown! It was one of the older homes and much better built than the shack we had formerly called home. We gained an attic, a cellar, smoke house, small barn and best of all <u>electricity!</u> There were also two lots with a large garden and several pear trees in the deal.

We had moved across Dutchtown, but the house would still be listed as semi-modern with 'six rooms and a path". We joined those neighborhood families who carried household water from the town pump just across the street, about the same distance as the faucet in Auggy's basement. The water was very good and some who used the well carried water buckets farther than a city block. One of my several chores was to keep the kitchen water bucket full and carry in the bath and wash water. Dad invested in two new galvanized buckets and promised I would be much stronger for golf. I labored hard to fill those ten gallon galvanized tubs for Saturday night baths and Monday's wash day. There is no record of how many hundred gallons of water I carried during the six years at 18th and E Streets, before I went to work for Uncle Sam. Although we lived inside the city limits for thirteen years, an outhouse on the alley was standard. Our family never lived in a house with indoor plumbing until after I was drafted. Low rent houses included an outhouse, but there was no charge for the exercise.

I recently had the opportunity to tour the old house while it was being remodeled by a new owner. It was a great experience to see the changes they had made. Warm boyhood memories of seventy-eight years ago came back quickly and for a brief time I was a teenager standing in the Past. The carpenter was a WW II buff and I sold him a book before I drove back into the present. City officials capped the well and removed the pump a few years after WW II, but the concrete base remains on the northeast corner of 18th and E Streets. Dad could have bought the place for eight hundred dollars, but that was a lot of money for a man earning $1.50 an hour.

The new feature I considered my personal reward was a big brown enameled heating stove sitting in the middle of the living room. The monster burned fuel oil and there were no ashes! Just like that, I had been freed from the chores of carrying coal to feed a pot-bellied stove all winter. Dad said it would heat the whole house which could mean fewer 'three dog nights' next winter. That was good because we were down to two dogs, Zero and Bootsie. Of course, I still had to keep the wood box full for Mom's kitchen range, but my school workload had been cut in half. Mom said it would give more time for sixth grade homework.

The Atwater-Kent radio was a great improvement which brought news and entertainment to our new house. Early on, in the little house, we had an old battery radio with a separate speaker horn, but Dad seldom had the money for the big six volt dry battery for power, so that radio sat silent in a back room. It was great that we moved to a house with electricity and could enjoy radio programs and news on our floor model Atwater-Kent radio. The family gathered around in the evenings to hear the news and favorite programs like Lum and Abner, Amos and Andy, Fibber Mc Gee and Molly, and Charlie Mc Carthy. I spent many evenings listening to radio serials like Little Orphan Annie and Dick Tracy. President Franklin D. Roosevelt held 'Fireside Chats' on the economy and Walter Winchell reported on the war clouds gathering in Europe and Asia. Politicians warned of an unstable world and a few years later, news reporters and patriotic movies flooded the airways to keep folks at home informed on the war. We were soon in WW II and movies flooded the screens urging folks at home, from defense plant workers to school children to buy War Bonds and support the boys in battle. No one imagined television in the home, except in the movies and that was only in Buck Rogers and Flash Gordon movie serials on Saturday afternoon. Radio by voice and Morse code messages were the main means of communication for land, sea and air combat. I enrolled in a Bedford High radio class in my senior year. A few months after graduation, I qualified for radio technical school and flew twenty missions as B-17 Radio operator/gunner in the Eighth Army Air Corps.

We had moved uptown or at least four blocks closer, seven years had passed, but we were still on the wrong side of the tracks. The depression was in full force and the struggle for money, food and clothing continued. Mom and Pop groceries allowed folks to run a 'bill' until payday, delivered grocery orders to the house and gave kids a treat when the bill was paid. Some were forced to close when bills weren't paid, it was hard to say no to a family with small children. There were seventy-five Mom and Pop neighborhood grocery stores in our small town in the mid '30's. Dry goods for home cooking and baking were the most common supplies. People found various ways to put food on the table. They preferred to work for food instead of asking the Township Trustee or local Welfare Department for a 'bean order.' Most families could only afford meat one day a week, unless they hunted, fished or raised their own livestock. Chickens, rabbits, pigs and cows were some of the critters raised to supplement the family diet. A henhouse and chicken coop in the backyard were common in those days. Chickens required very little room and the by-product was great fertilizer for the garden. You didn't need an alarm clock with all those chickens in the neighborhood. The roosters made sure everyone in the area was awake at sunrise. Eggs and an occasional fried chicken were important food for a growing family and a big old fat hen made a fine family dinner. Chicken and dumplins' was a Sunday dinner to remember all week long. Surplus eggs, milk, or meat could be traded or sold to neighbors or local grocery stores.

Our Barn

The barn on the alley was a miniature of a much bigger one complete with two stalls, a hayloft and a chicken coop. All of which had been used by the previous owner for milk cows and chickens. Dad didn't have time for a cow, but several unemployed or retired neighbors kept one or two in sheds on the alley. Early every morning they led a cow or two in a parade down E street to Wray's pasture where they could graze all day for a reasonable fee. (Lincoln School now stands on that land) The caravan was reversed in the evening when they were led back to cow sheds for food and milking. The pasture was a bargain and they only bought hay for winter months. Neighborhood women along the route called it the 'Stinky Cow- Cow Boogie' because the lumbering beasts often left smelly deposits in the street.

Our family never went into the dairy business, Dad had spent too many years milking cows on the farm and Mom was not about to join the daily Cow Parades. That decision allowed me to use the barn as a henhouse and suddenly, I was in the egg business. Aunt Gladys and Uncle Ray left the farm to manage a Cream Station in town. Frosty was not too happy about that, but later helped Uncle Ray run routes over country roads to buy milk, cream, chickens and eggs to sell to a local dairy and grocery stores. They bought large flocks of chickens and culled out the weak or unhealthy hens they could not send to market. Uncle Ray gave those to me to feed and promised to buy them when and if they recovered. Our vacant barn became a chicken coop and I became the caretaker of a flock of scrawny chickens to nurse back to health. I built an outside pen to give them sunshine and buried my failures in the garden. Later, I was surprised by an extra bonus when some hens began laying eggs! I had not counted on getting a cash crop, but I built a row of box nests in the barn. Uncle Ray gave me a rooster and I collected eggs like Uncle Clark down on the farm. Some of my chicken feed came from a federal government program set up in 1939 to distribute surplus food to needy families. Our family qualified, even though Dad had a WPA job. Mom and I stood in long lines each month to receive food such as dry beans, canned beef, rice, peanut butter, several grapefruits and a sack of flour. The flour sometimes had weevils in it, Mom said our family was usually hungry, but not that hungry, so I fed it to my chickens. My hens loved the small worms and their eggs never had weevils. Eventually, I owned a flock of healthy hens and one happy rooster. I think protein from the weevils did the trick! The egg business went so well that I decided to keep all the chickens and sell the eggs. Our cellar gave me cool storage and Dad was my biggest customer. When the family needed a dozen eggs, he handed me fifteen cents to go across the street to Loudens grocery. I was out the back door in a flash, but never went to the store. I scrambled down to the cellar and carefully sacked the eggs for delivery upstairs. I'm sure didn't fool Dad and he probably had a big laugh at my first business venture. The egg business became too much trouble and I felt guilty, so gave the egg business to Jean and Kenny. They sent all eggs directly to Mom's kitchen and I went to hunt another job. Luckily, Uncle Ray bought all the chickens before winter came upon the land and I was years ahead of Colonel Sanders.

Victory gardens were very necessary to meet the food shortages in World War II and rationing stamps were issued for items like meat and sugar. People took great pride in their backyard vegetable gardens. Vacant lots were rented for a share of the harvest. Those gardens provided food for the table and canned goods for the winter during those trying times when families struggled to make ends meet. Children were expected to do their part and every kid in the gang had household chores to finish before he was free to play. Mom had a house to run and Dad was out on a job or looking for work. Kids worked before they played and we grew up knowing that work was a fact of life. We spent many long hours hoeing and weeding in gardens. Harvesting the crops was a happier chore, but I hated the back-breaking task of picking beans and peas. Guess I was just not cut out to be a pea picker!

Few families gave children an allowance, but people in the neighborhood would pay for jobs like running errands, picking fruit, raking leaves or lawn mowing. A kid could pick up a little money that way and we soon learned that it was important to have the reputation as a good worker. One summer Old Lady Cooper hired me and Chad to pick cherries. She had several trees of ripe cherries, but the birds were getting most of the harvest. She liked to work early in the morning to beat the heat. Rickety ladders and a cranky old lady below pointing out every cherry you missed made for a hectic morning. She paid us five cents a gallon and it was hard-earned money, but we were glad to get it. Good paying jobs like that were short and hard to find. I helped Tuffy on his paper route for a while, but most days I was free to find my next adventure and a big one happened later that summer when Dad got me my first caddy job at the Otis Park golf course. Doc and Chad were already working there and Skinny and Tuffy came out on weekends. We made a little money and learned how to work, but it sure cut into our free time.

"The best thing about the future is that it comes one day at a time.
Abraham Lincoln

Huckster Wagons

The large Louden's Grocery across the street from House #2 was one of many family owned grocery stores in Bedford. They also served customers by traveling county roads with three 'huckster wagons' running different routes five days a week. The store allowed credit to its country customers so families could 'run a bill' for groceries as long as they paid up every week or two according to agreement. Huckster wagons were a long-established business which began in the horse and buggy days when most farm families only came to town to 'trade' on Saturday. General stores in the county and small towns offered a limited supply of groceries and supplies and enterprising peddlers outfitted a wagon with goods and groceries, hitched up the horse and peddled their wares to families in rural areas. In the mid 1930s, the Loudens grocery owners purchased three old school buses, tore out the seats and installed bins and shelves to hold groceries. Their 'Huckster Wagons' were literally stores on wheels designed to cover rural routes five days a week selling groceries, kerosene and sacks of feed. The driver could accept eggs, chickens or produce as payment and each bus had a rear platform to hold a kerosene barrel and one or two wooden chicken coops. The big store was an important source of income for Dutchtown teenagers, because it had so many part-time jobs. Their warehouse was great place to loaf and maybe earn a little money re-stocking the huckster wagons, delivering orders or unloading trucks in late afternoon.

Country General Store   Library of Congress

We watched for the huckster wagon's return in the afternoon because drivers sold crème-filled day-old Twinkies and Cupcakes for a nickel. It was a great bargain even though they had been on the hot truck all day. Nobody got sick, except one afternoon when Skinny ate too many. We also watched because we might get a job. The driver often bought or traded for farm produce, like vegetables or chickens and had to go back out with a truck to pick it up. We were in luck if he bought chickens because he hired two or three of us to go out at night to catch them roosting (sleeping). It was an opportunity to earn a little spending money, but it was a rough job to slip into a pitch black hen house. Blindly grabbing sleeping chickens off a perch and cramming them into a wooden crate was not an easy job. The driver chose the hard job of holding the door until we had all the victims in the crates. We tried to capture as many sleepers as possible. Chasing squawking chickens through a henhouse in the flickering shadows of a farmer's lantern is not fun. One night Tuffy fell on the messy floor and the driver made him ride home in the back of the truck with the chicken crates. They also hired us to 'kill and dress' chickens to sell in their meat department on weekends. The task of part-time chicken plucker was not my favorite job, we were paid a pittance to kill chickens, toss them into a vat of scalding hot water, pull them out and pluck off all feathers. At that point, the store's butcher took over and the Health Department was never involved.

We had moved up town, or at least four blocks closer andseven years had passed, but we were still on the wrong side of the tracks. The depression was in full force and the struggle for money, food and clothing continued. Dry goods for home cooking and baking were the most common supplies. People found various ways to put food on the table. They preferred to work for food instead of asking the Township Trustee or local Welfare Department for a 'bean order.' Most families could only afford meat one day a week, unless they hunted, fished or raised their own livestock. Chickens, rabbits, pigs and cows were some of the critters raised to supplement the family diet. A henhouse and chicken coop in the backyard were common in those days. Chickens required very little room and the by-product was great fertilizer for the garden. You didn't need an alarm clock with all those chickens in the neighborhood. The roosters made sure everyone in the area was awake at sunrise. Eggs and an occasional fried chicken were important food for a growing family and a big old fat hen made a fine family dinner. Chicken and dumplins' was a Sunday dinner to remember all week long. Surplus eggs, milk, or meat could be traded or sold to neighbors or local grocery stores.

Abel's Blacksmith Shop

There was a lot of noisy and explosive action in our new neighborhood and it came from a very active blacksmith forge just across the alley behind our barn. Anytime we heard the clanging of metal on metal, we knew Tom Abel and his two young sons, Marshall and Dutch were busy heating, making or repairing everything from plow shares to horseshoes.

140

The blacksmith shop was an intriguing hang- out for boys to watch strong men work on a wide variety of broken items customers brought in for repair. Of course, the blacksmith shop and alley was out of bounds to kids, but we had ringside seats any day of the week by climbing a ladder inside our barn and sitting in the barn loft window. We had reserved seats in the balcony ten foot above the hectic action with a panoramic view of the alley and forge.

A steady flow of horses and wagons, trucks and farm equipment visited the shop on the alley between 18th and 19th streets. Sparks flew and flamed blazed when the blacksmith loaded the forge with coke and pumped the bellows for red hot coals. They hammered glowing red metal into horse shoes and installed or parts for farm machinery. Their main tools were the orange red fire in the forge, tongs, hammers, anvils and muscles. They were experienced blacksmiths with talent and strength. They made or invented parts needed for farm or industrial equipment. Their hard labor was often accompanied by loud yelling and singing (ears take a beating in a blacksmith shop). Sometimes there was a some cussing when things went wrong.

Farmers unhitched horses from the buggy or wagon and tied them to our fence to cool down from the trip into town. We were free to pet or feed them hanks of grass while they waited for 'new shoes.' Eventually, the blacksmith came for the horse, led him to the proper area horse and tied him securely. Horse hooves outgrew shoes every few months and old horses were accustomed to being shod. It is not too hard to shoe a gentle horse, if it co-operates. Horses' hooves need to be trimmed and shod regularly so they were used to the routine. The blacksmith's normal procedure was to lift to the left front leg, clamp it between knees, remove the worn shoe and trim the hoof. Next, he measured the hoof so he could repair or replace the shoe, heat and shape the red hot shoe on the anvil, cool it and nail it back on the hoof. Of course, he had to do that four times!

The Blacksmith Shop had an interesting by-product to benefit their neighbors. It was the water from their quenching tub by the red fire. All red hot iron pieces were dipped and cooled (quenched) in that tub of water. The oxidized water would cure Poison Ivy and adults and kids often came for a gallon of water from the quenching tub to cure the pesky itching. Time marches on, the blacksmith forges are out of business and horse shoeing is almost a lost art. Today, horses get their shoes from farriers who come to the farm in well equipped trucks to make 'barn calls'.

Note: Years later Marshall Abel and I played a lot of golf at Otis Park. The Bedford Library also recorded an interview of Marshall on his years as a blacksmith in Dutchtown.

They Rode Off in all Directions And They Went That-a-way!

Shoot' em up westerns at the Von Ritz, Indiana and Lawrence theaters were our favorite entertainment and Saturday matinees were a real bargain in those days before television. A dime bought a ticket for a Western, a 'B' movie (a low cost non-western), and best of all, another episode of an adventure serial! Serials were usually produced with twelve chapters of thrilling action. One fifteen-minute chapter was shown each week and always ended with the hero facing death in a hopeless situation. Of course, we all wanted to go back next Saturday to see if and how he escaped (he always did). It cost a dime to see the matinee in 1935, but a tender-hearted cashier at the Von Ritz theater would take my dime and let my little sister and brother in free. We were ages ten, seven and four and I remember the fateful day when a Jack Holt western was playing on Sunday afternoon and the three of us had the magic dime. We walked the eight blocks to the theater and the cashier had to turn us down. She said we were all getting too old. It was a long sad walk home and I never did get to see that western. Maybe TV will re-run it someday! Tickets were cheap, but it was pretty easy to sneak in if you didn't have a dime. Tuffy learned that older went behind the Lawrence theater and climbed a ladder up to the ventilating fans. Chad, Doc, Tubby and I did it on a dare a few times, but crawling through those fan blades was scary and stupid. We quit because it was dangerous, but we also we knew we would get 'whuppins' if our dads found out about it. You had to be careful, when tattletales like Maudie's gang were around!

Movie cowboys were our heroes and we had favorites to imitate with our 'cap' guns and stick horses. A box of caps (five rolls) was only a nickel, so we had lots of noise to make our cowboy battles more realistic. Westerns had plenty of chase scenes, except they were stagecoaches and covered wagons. The majority of the low budget films were made on studio 'back lots.' During those years we watched our hero race past the same scenery in film after film! We never questioned how the horse could run forever and his six- shooter could fire twenty times. However, around the ages of thirteen, we began to wonder why in the world the hero kiss the pretty girl and ride off into the sunset.

Our favorite matinee idols were Tom Mix, Buck Jones, Ken Maynard and Tim McCoy who was awarded the Bronze Star in World War II. Buck Jones and his horse, Silver starred in many movies and serials and I tried to see all of them. Ken and Buck were my favorites because they were Hoosiers. Buck's hometown was Columbus and Ken was from the Ft. Wayne area. Bob Steele was another Saturday matinee hero. He was very athletic and rode like the wind on his horse, Pal. Once his 'hero' days were over, he became a character actor and appeared in big name westerns for many years.

We could never forget our experience with Tom Mix the day his circus came to Bedford. We donned our cowboy hats, pinned on our Tom Mix Straight Shooters badges and stood in front of the crowd to see him in the Circus Parade to the Fairgrounds. Lo and behold, the famous western star, riding Tony the Wonder Horse, passed within four feet of us and waved. Not one of us money for a ticket but we were so sure he was waving at us that we decided to go out to the Fairgrounds for a chance to see him again. That idea didn't pan out, so we decided to sneak in the back way. We went behind the Big Top and crawled under a canvas partition, stood up and our hero less than twenty feet from us. He was relaxing in a hammock between shows and Tony was tied nearby, munching hay. We were thrilled when the famous Western star sat up and spoke to us. We hoped he might let us in free, but hero said in a very in a firm voice he,

"You kids get out of here right now!"

I led our hasty retreat back under the canvas. We had broken the Tom Mix Club Motto:

Straight Shooters always win, lawbreakers always lose.

Several western stars visited Bedford in the thirties, I couldn't afford most of them, but I once paid two bits to see Ken Maynard and his wonder Horse, Tarzan, on stage at the Indiana Theater. The Sons of the Pioneers western singing group once came to town and stayed at the Greystone Hotel. My buddies and I were loafing in front of the poolroom on the north side of the square when they walked past to eat at a café that sold beer and we were really let down!

They say, what goes around comes around and I recently had that experience with an old western re-run. The television program was a 1935 John Wayne western titled 'The Star Packer'. The very same western I saw at the Von Ritz at the age of ten when the admission was one thin dime! This time, in 2016, I viewed it on a $400 television set with a $145.00 monthly program charge!

I recently visited the old Lawrence Theater building and the stage remains in the rear of what is now Crane's Western Store. The owner showed me a hole in the stage which was punched out by the hoof of a 'Wonder Horse' of a touring western star many years ago.

I remember many of the Saturday matinee western heroes of my generation and names of their horses! They taught us right from wrong. The good guys wore white hats and defeated rustlers wearing black. Tom Mix was one of the first early movie heroes to promote good behavior. The motto of his Tom Mix Club was basic,

'Straight Shooters always win, lawbreakers always lose'.

Everybody in the gang mailed two Post Toasty box tops to become upstanding Straight Shooters. We were a sad bunch seven year old kids when Von Ritz theater burned in 1932, but repairs were made quickly and it operated for many years as an entertainment center for kids and adults.

The Snipe Hunt

Snipe hunting was a popular night time sport with Dutchtown teenagers in 1938. It was also one of the biggest 'con games' carried out by teenagers. Hunting for small game was a normal practice in our neighborhood. It was necessary activity to supplement the family diet. However, snipe hunts weren't scheduled too often because they usually resulted in a 'ruckus' among parents. The hunt organizer's first step was to find a kid who had never been snipe hunting (usually someone new to the neighborhood) and invite him to join them on a big hunt. The new kid was made to feel privileged to be included in this secret activity with his new friends. He was sworn to secrecy and warned to tell no one, especially his parents, about the big event. Meanwhile, his new buddies talked a lot about the prospect of catching a record number of snipe!

A snipe hunt was a simple operation with few requirements, a moonless night, flashlights, and a large grass-sack (burlap bag). When the night of the big hunt arrived, the gang of teenagers quietly moved into the dark woods to an open space in an area where snipe had been recently seen. The new boy, the guest of honor, was given the most important task of trapping the snipes. His job was to stand in the middle of the dark clearing and hold the grass-sack wide open to catch the birds as they fled to escape the bright lights. He didn't need a flashlight, it would scare the birds. The hunt consisted of everybody else spreading out in the dark to form a ring around the clearing. These guys were to move in waving their flashlights to tighten the circle and scare the snipe into the clearing. The guys in the woods shined their lights for a while as they tightened the circle, but at a given signal, the lights went out and there was complete darkness! The unsuspecting victim was left 'holding the bag'. Everyone waited for the reactions of the 'new kid' when he realized he was the butt of a carefully planned hoax and had no way to find his way out of the dark woods without a flashlight! He also knew that he had a lot of pleading and begging to do before the flashlights would light up the woods again.

The outcome of the post-hunt 'hullabaloo' depended on how the victim accepted the practical joke. Eventually, most kids laughed, joined in the joke and become one of the gang. The cry-baby who ran to complain to his parents, started a real neighborhood rumble. The fight often started that same night or early the next morning, depending on how vividly the pathetic victim told his story and how strongly his folks confronted the parents of the kids involved and demanded justice. The guilty culprits got a trip to the woodshed and there were a lot of sore backsides in Dutchtown for a few days. The cry-baby became a 'kid without a gang' and was shunned by the other guys.

Generally, it was quite a while before another snipe hunt was organized!

The encyclopedia describes the snipe as a type of marsh bird of the sandpiper family. However, there is no record of a snipe being trapped in a sack held by a scared teenager in a dark Indiana woods."

The Dutchtown Cave

I heard about the Dutchtown cave with three 'stone saddles' deep inside from guys in our sixth grade class at Lincoln school before we moved from the south-end to the center of Dutchtown. The cave was just a block from our new home at 18th and E Streets and being an avid Western fan, I was determined to see those 'saddles' as soon as possible. My first priority was to cultivate some new friends to induct me into the 'brotherhood of the cave.' I soon found guys my age who had explored the cave and they were more than willing to show me its wonders.

The cave was is in a low area at the base of a hill near the corner of 18th and D Streets behind the Hutton boys' house. Tuffy had a great basketball court in his backyard on the corner, but the Huttons had the cave! We had enough daylight in the entrance that we could store our torches on a dry ledge. The lights were torches made with whiskey bottles half-filled with kerosene. The wick was a twisted rag stuffed tightly down the bottleneck. Some guys brought flashlights, but mostly we used the Dutchtown version of a 'Molotov Cocktail' like the Russians later used against tanks in WWII. Actually, the torches were accidents waiting to happen and we were really lucky that none exploded. We realized the danger of losing a torch and being trapped in pitch-black darkness. We used the buddy system when exploring and there was a strict rule that no kid could enter the cave alone. Our gang made many explorations deep into the cave with those dangerous torches in 1936-40. Caves have constant temperatures between 49- 52 degrees, so our cave was cool in the summer and warm in the winter. It was used when the weather hampered outdoor activities with snow, rain or the dog days of summer and great for crawling through the dark while holding a flaming bottle of kerosene. Summer days, we enjoyed the cool temperature of the cave by exploring or sitting just inside the entrance. The reverse was true on cold winter days when school didn't interrupt our free time. We knew inside the cave would be warmer and/ or we could build a fire in the large entrance.

The cave had several large chambers as we moved deeper and we often had to squeeze through narrow passages or crawl through tunnels on our hands and knees to reach them. It fact, fat kids or adults seldom reached some of those rooms. The famous 'saddle room' was more than a hundred feet from the entrance. It could only be reached by wiggling through a few narrow openings on your belly which wasn't an easy task with a torch in your hand. One thing you didn't do was crowd too close to the guy ahead because you might give him a real hotfoot or worse. Of course, if you were leading, you made sure the guy behind was aware of that fact. When we reached our goal, we could sit on the three rounded stone formations formed by centuries of erosion, but only a teenager's imagination would have called them 'saddles.'

We wrote our names on the cave roof with black smoke from the torch or scratched them on the soft sandy walls. Farther beyond the beyond the saddle room the cave had three levels. At one point there was a crevice and we could hear a fairly large stream of water running below. We knew the hole was deep because when you dropped a rock it took a long time to hear a splash. It was tempting, but needless to say, we never tried to climb down to those lower levels. Crawling into and through narrow openings to get to the various dry sections at our own level was enough of a challenge.

We didn't want our parents to know about our caving expeditions, but clothing tends to get dusty or muddy when you're crawling around deep in a cave. However, there was a solution for that problem in the summer, because we could go over behind Hutton's house. Their parents worked and there was an outdoor faucet where we could wash the dirt off our clothes to destroy the evidence!

There were bats in the cave, but we seldom encountered them on the top level and in those days, nobody said anything about them having rabies. So we were blissfully ignorant of that danger. Some nights when things were slow, we sat on Tuffy's' basketball court to watch them fly out to dine on the local flying insects. That was also a good time to throw a cap in the air and watch them dive after it. Many people believed bats only came out at night because they could not see in daylight. One summer day Chad, Tuffy and I discovered a bat hanging from the ceiling of the saddle room. We trapped the sleeping critter in one of my socks and decided our captive was the perfect subject to discover the truth. Our plan for the scientific 'bat eyesight' experiment was simple, but Chad said we needed witnesses to verify our findings. We took it up to the front porch of Loudens grocery across from my house where some of the other guys were loafing in the shade. Our timing was perfect, it was high noon on a sunny day and we were more than a block away from the cave. Several adults joined us and offered opinions, some said the bat could see, others said he couldn't. Everyone was anxious to see who was right and interest was high when we released the captive. It was a short scientific event. That bat made one high circle, dipped low and flew a bee-line straight back to his home in the cave and thus ended our use of the old saying, "He's as blind as a bat!"

No one ever called us spelunkers but we were, and very lucky ones to boot! Today the cave entrance is sealed by a wall of stone half way up the hillside and not even a bat can get inside. There is little evidence that it ever existed, but even sadder is the fact that very few of those boys who played in the Dutchtown Cave seventy-five years to eighty years ago are living today.

Blue Hole

The depression ruined the stone industry, abandoned stone quarries were scattered throughout the county and most were very deep and full of sky blue water. However, we had our own Blue Hole in town at the north end of 'F' street. It was less than six blocks from our neighborhood which was closer than the city pools or Leatherwood

Creek and we could ride our bikes right up to the edge of this one. We realized that quarry swimming without lifeguards was dangerous and only suitable for strong swimmers because most holes had steep stone walls which limited entrance and exit from the water. Several drownings were blamed on poor swimmers attempting more than possible or good swimmers getting muscle cramps in the deep cold water. The main attractions of Blue Holes were that they made great skinny-dippin' swimming pools and were free.

Our in-town Blue Hole was a small quarry with high walls on only two sides, but those stretched thirty feet up the woods. The big attractions were the facts that it was small with an easy way to get in or out of the water and a tall limestone island in the middle. Owners had stacked large blocks of stone to make a tall tower in the middle of the quarry while it was still in operation and that stack became an island when underground springs and rainwater filled the abandoned hole in the earth. The 'limestone tower island' made our Blue Hole special because we only needed to swim a short distance to crawl on to it at water level. It was far enough into the woods to allow skinny dippin' and a perfect spot to enjoy swimming, diving or just sunning on the rocks with the big boys. Swimming a while to cool off and stretching out on a stone block to tan awhile was a summer day well spent. Once you were 'well done,' spaces among the huge blocks of stacked stone provided cool shady nooks to escape more rays of the hot summer sun.

The island also provided an opportunity for the daring adventures of underwater swimming and high diving. Both activities were great for teenagers and young men who were strong swimmers and enjoyed a challenge. Spaces between the stacked limestone blocks had created a twenty foot tunnel about six feet underwater. That was another challenge to add to your 'brag list' and we swam the tunnel often. Holding my breath for that distance was no problem, but it was about the same as going into a cave. The thrill was in knowing that once you entered, you were in danger until you swam all the way through the enclosed space. We always had a guy on top the tower to watch the swimmer go under and run to the other side to make sure he came out safely. Swimming through the underwater tunnels was for daredevils and good swimmers.

Projecting stones gave us various heights of ledges for diving but high diving from the top level took nerve and skill because it was about twenty feet above the water. A diver needed strong legs to push out and away from the stone wall. Jumping or diving from the north side of the island was safest because the wall was straighter up and down and there were no stone blocks hidden underwater to bang your skull.

The greatest diving challenge was from the north wall that soared up to the woods and only a few dared to do it. Most of us had agreed that it was one fine challenge to ignore. But Chad was the daredevil of our gang and we were not too surprised one day in our 1939 summer when he made his announcement,

"Guys, I think I'm gon'na try diving from the woods."

Doc said, "Ya better not, ya might go too deep, hit a rock and break an arm, then no basketball team."

I chimed in with, "Yes, and ya might hit your head on a rock, why don't you jump the first time."

Tuffy and Skinny warned against it too, but he had made up his mind and all we could was sit on the island and watch him climb buck naked up through woods to reach the spot other divers used. He got set, didn't hesitate and launched out into space in a graceful swan dive to split the water perfectly. We were afraid he went too deep and he did! He came up close to the island holding his forehead. He had gone deep enough to graze a rock and was bleeding badly. We helped our buddy climb up on the island and Doc swam over to get our shirts for bandages. We cleaned the cut, luckily it was not too deep and we got the bleeding stopped before we all went to his house to help explain his head wound to his parents. Chad had learned a lesson the hard way and he later admitted that we were right to try and talk him from the high dive. He assured us it was his last one from the woods.

The island created problems because there were so many poor swimmers getting into trouble. There were reports of a couple of near-drownings every summer and more than one kid had to be dragged out of our Blue Hole. Our second big event that summer happened when Doc's cousin Leroy came to visit for a week a week before school started. Every kid in our gang was a strong swimmer qualified for the quarry. We were leery of taking poor swimmers to the Blue Hole without lifeguards. We usually took them to down to a Leatherwood Creek swimming hole like Sycamore or Nine Foot. We weren't crazy about taking Leroy to Blue Hole so we swam in Leatherwood and took him in the cave. However, Cousin Leroy was from Muncie, up north, and didn't want to go home go home until he could brag about swimming in a Southern Indiana quarry hole. The skinny little kid was not a strong swimmer in the creek but he assured us he would be okay in Blue Hole. The afternoon crowd was light and Leroy's adventure was going smoothly until the imp decided to jump off the top without telling anyone. Doc saw him just as he jumped and was sure he scrapped his butt on the wall going down. He hit the water flat on his belly and face. That knocked the breath out of him. He panicked and came up screaming for help and flailing the water like a wounded duck. Tuffy yelled for everyone to be careful going in to drag him out because he might pull a rescuer under with him. Chad and Tuffy stayed on the island to anchor themselves while three of us went in to get him. We made a sort of chain of arms. I held on to Tuffy's hand and reached out to Skinny , who reached out to Doc while he managed to grab his cousin's arm. We all pulled him back against the island to pull and push him to safety. It took a half hour or so to calm down Leroy and convince him that he could swim the short distance from the island to the shore.

That episode ended Cousin Leroy's Blue Hole experience. He went home with a sore butt and the knowledge that he was not ready for quarry swimming. I doubt that he ever bragged about it up North!

Old Cement Plant

The long abandoned United States Cement Company was east of town on Leatherwood Road. It once consisted of ten large buildings, various sheds and several 'company houses' for workers. The narrow stone road wound down the Slaughterhouse Hill and over the Arched Stone bridge for about two miles along Leatherwood Creek. Information in James Guthrie's 'Lawrence County History' reports the plant operated for several years before closing in 1909. The railroad tore out the spur line and bridge over Leatherwood Creek and the company jobs were gone with the wind. Sometimes we found rusty railroad spikes or a piece of steel in the old abandoned roadbed that ran through the tunnel past Uncle Billy's farm toward White River. The owners sold most of the buildings and equipment for salvage, but the remaining ruins became a valuable asset to Dutchtown kids. The large deserted plant provided an intriguing playground with remnants of brick hearths, tunnels and out-buildings to explore.

Rairden's Hilltop Diary stored large stacks of hay in one barn-like building and that was an added bonus. Haystacks are special, they smell clean and retain the warm rays of summer. They are a great attraction for boys of all ages, especially when they can climb up on rafters and practice 'belly buster' dives. Jumping into loose hay or burrowing in a warm haystack was a great way to spend a cold or rainy day. Sunny days, we also enjoyed digging and leaping off the large sand bank south of the plant. We played many days in those long deserted cement plant buildings. It was an interesting and amazing playground to roam and explore; sort of a rustic Disney World. However, it all came to a screeching halt one winter day when the building and hay was destroyed in a fire. Suddenly, there were 'No Trespassing' signs nailed up all over the place and our days of romping through the ruins of the old cement plant were over!

Cabin in the Woods

We found other places to play on rainy days and later in the summer some of the older guys told us about the sand banks and a deserted limestone quarry which had provided the limestone for making cement. We knew about the sand banks, now we would see where they quarried the most important ingredient for making cement. The land behind the plant was not 'posted' so we followed an old road into the woods and our search was easy because no amount of brush or trees can hide a Southern Indiana stone quarry. Thousands of tons of limestone had been drilled or blasted out of a hillside and loaded on wagons with teams of horses or mules to haul down to the plant. We were amazed at size and realized that before us stood an opportunity for an entirely new adventure, because we saw a high stone cliff just begging to be climbed. We accepted the challenge, but not before we did a careful survey to decide on the safest place to climb to the top. Chad led the way, finding safe hand and footholds as we carefully pulled our way upward, over rocks and debris. Our dogs did their best to follow and were frustrated at being left behind. We ignored their barking and whining to focus on a safe climb. No one noticed when they stopped. We were pooped by the time we reached the top but amazed that our four dogs were waiting to welcome us! They had simply searched and found a wagon road winding up the hill beside the quarry. We were tuckered out from climbing the cliff in the heat of mid-morning. It was definitely time for a break and we sprawled out in the shade to survey the country-side from our high perch.

Skinny made the important 'find' when he spotted a small building among the trees on the hillside opposite the quarry. It was a very interesting discovery which needed to be investigated as soon as we had the energy. At that point, we had a case of 'sanity' and agreed that going down the cliff would be more dangerous than climbing. Somebody could lose his grip and fall. Besides, it would take too much time, so we followed our dogs on their by-pass route down the road. The sun was low in the sky by the time we were back on the quarry floor. Our gang had climbed the cliff, now we were intrigued by the fact that the deserted building might make a cabin. However, we were running out of daylight and it would take time to locate the 'mystery building' building up on the hill. We postponed our search, followed the lane down past the cement plant, waded the creek and took the path back up through Glover's pasture to my house. Quick plans were made to meet early the next day to head back to the quarry with a sack lunch and full canteen. (Our canteens were pop bottles sealed with a cork stopper)

Next morning, we set up camp at the base of the hill opposite the quarry wall and made two unsuccessful searches across the hillside before our noon break. We were disappointed and frustrated, but not ready to say 'Uncle.' Skinny said his Dad thought it could be a shed quarrymen had used to store dynamite. He also suggested that we might try the 'line of sight' method. He said he would go back to the top of the cliff, locate the cabin and point the direction, Doc could stand half way across the quarry floor and point the same direction to the rest of us at the edge of the woods. Everybody agreed it was a heck of an idea, but only if Skinny took the quick easy road up the hillside. We shared our sack lunches with the dogs and Skinny took off while Doc moved out to climb a stack of rocks on the quarry floor. The plan would only work if Doc could see Skinny and we could see Doc. The dogs followed me, Chad and Tuffy to the woods at the bottom of the hill. We were surprised when Skinny and Doc lined it up, because it was much farther the left of the hillside we searched that morning. Skinny and Doc returned and we fanned out, moved up the hill and found the abandoned building with no trouble. It was half way up the hill on a flat spot surrounded by trees and brush. The 'cabin' was about the size of a small garage, half-buried in the hillside. It was a solid building with stone walls, dirt floor, rusty roof and a metal door dangling on one hinge. It was an exciting discovery with scads of possibilities without a lot of repair. Climbing the hill in the afternoon heat called for a break. The dogs joined us after they had a drink and cooled off in the small spring at the foot of the hill. We rested in the deep shade before checking inside the cabin. Of course, the water in our home-made canteens was warm, but at least it was wet. Every kid had an idea on ways to use our discovery and how great it would be to have a secret cabin in the woods. It was a place we could build a campfire and stay dry in wet or cold weather. Curiosity shortened our restbreak and we headed for the 'grand opening'.

During the break, we had agreed that Skinny should have the honor of being first to enter, but before he stepped through the door, Doc reminded him to watch for snakes. Skinny stopped short and immediately declined the great honor he had been given. The possibility of snakes had not been a topic of discussion. There was an awkward pause until Tuffy picked up a stick and volunteered to lead us inside the dim lit building. Suddenly our dogs became really excited about getting inside. Tuffy pulled open the sagging door, it fell off its hinges and all four dogs dashed in to surround a pile of boards and rusty tin in a dark corner of the room. The dogs were barking wildly as Tuffy poked his stick at the boards. Pandemonium reigned when two fat copperhead snakes slithered out across the floor to crawl into a crevice in the stone wall! The frustrated dogs clawed at the hole in the wall while five terrified boys made a mad scramble for the door and safety in the shady rest area. We held a short conference and quickly agreed a cabin in the woods was not such a good idea after all. Five boys and four dogs were soon making tracks down the hill for home. The abandoned dynamite cabin was left to the poisonous copperheads. That Dutchtown adventure ended with: Chad proud he led us up the cliff; Skinny proud he found the cabin; Doc proud he warned of snakes; Tuffy proud he poked them out; I was just glad to be home.

Dreams of having cabin of our own quickly evaporated --- as dreams often do!

Basketball Hoops

Basketball, the Indiana state game, was our major sport and outdoor courts were all over town in backyards, playgrounds and parks. They ranged from a hoop nailed to the side of a barn to formal blacktop courts with regulation goals. School playgrounds featured a regulation court for neighborhood teams and basketball games were the main activity as Phys. Ed. in Jr. High and High School gyms. Coaches often gave used balls to talented youngsters who couldn't afford one to practice at home. A basketball was a prized gift and any kid who owned a regulation ball was welcomed with open arms and a new basketball was a season ticket to about any playground. Most kids were serious about improving skills and practiced dribbling skills and sound of a bouncing basketball echoed in the neighborhood as they went down sidewalks to various courts. Most boys were pretty good players, but not good enough to try-out for a team. Dutchtown scrimmage and pick-up games were more fun and we spent many hours in competition. We learned to choose sides and win or lose without mental anguish and parents, cheerleaders or trophies were not involved. However, parents were happy to know where their kids were; some even rigged lights for night games. In reality, many of us were just too busy to spend our time in organized teams which usually cost money. We joined the Thornton Boys Club, membership was a dime, but it was too far across the tracks to go to play basketball.

We liked Tuffy's half-court down near the cave, after a hard game on hot days we could sit in the cave entrance to cool off. His court was usually ignored by older and better players. They liked the big blacktop full court behind the Louden grocery. It was shorter than regulation but had goals, with nets, at each end! Old Man Louden built it as a community project for Dutchtown boys and young men. He told his customers,

"Well, I figure they might as well be playing basketball as loafing around and getting' in trouble."

The big full court was a tremendous success and we had a lot of Dutchtown players make the teams and star at school or the Boys Cub. Skinny, Tuffy and Chad became pretty good players as they grew older. Doc and I were more interested in golf at Otis Park and were often chosen last for pick-up games. Skinny eventually became our gang's tallest and most talented players and starred on our Bedford High team, the Stonecutters.

They played in the State Tourney Finals in 1943,our senior year when our country was deep into World War II and gasoline was rationed. Chad's mother volunteered to drive us the seventy-five miles to Indianapolis if she could collect enough gas stamps from parents. Our seats were down front; we cheered madly for our buddy and the Stonecutters, but lost by a few points in the afternoon semi-final game.

Mitchell High had gone to the finals in 1940. Lawrence County had twelve High Schools and many graduates played on college teams. The Torphy brothers, John and Bill, were members of the 1940 Indiana University which won the National Championship team. Fred Beretta played four years at Purdue and was an All-American. Fred went overseas on the Queen Mary, I know that, because I found his name carved in the handrail when I went over months later. In the past few years our Bedford-North Lawrence boy's team has won the State and our girl's team has won the State Tourney three times.

My trip to the State Finals was a great day in May of 1943 and I was the farthest I had ever been from home. Of course, I had no idea I would be sitting in Army barracks at Amarillo, Texas three months later.

"I had been caught in the draft and was a thousand miles from Bedford High School with no diploma!"

Chapter 8

Fred B. Otis—Dutchtown Neighbor

Fred Bishop Otis was no stranger to Dutchtown kids. He was born and grew up in the neighborhood. The long time owner and publisher of the Bedford Daily Mail and his sister, Francis Zara Otis, lived in a big house on the corner of 22nd and H Streets and we knew them as adults who liked school kids. Zara was a pleasant lady who loved working in the flower garden covering the front yard down to the sidewalk. She often spoke or waved as we passed on our way to or from school. Tulips and Dahlias were her favorite seasonal flowers and some days she gave each of us one to take to our teacher. We seldom saw Mr. Otis anywhere but his small newspaper building on east Sixteenth Street (site of present Times-Mail) but that was easy because it had a huge glass window facing the street so people interested in printing presses could stand and watch the large monster in operation any afternoon. Later I got a bike and paper route and often watched the old editor supervise the day's issue of all the news fit to print while I waited to pick up my papers in the area next to the Salvation Army House. We made door to door delivery, collected the ten cent subscription fee on Friday and made three cents unless some customers didn't pay.

The former owner of the Bedford Daily Mail bought the Bedford Country Club, the Civil War era mansion, Pine Hall, and one hundred and forty-five acres and donated it to the city October, 1935. He specified that Otis Park was to be dedicated to refined recreation and pleasure for all the people of Bedford, especially those in his own eastside neighborhood of Dutchtown. The boys in our gang were young, but we realized the importance of the huge gift of Mr. Otis when the news was announced

The gift listed specific items for the city to construct additional facilities in the park and up-grade the country club swimming pool and Pine Hall mansion. Mr. Otis loved music and included a requirement for a beautiful Limestone Band Shell to be constructed in near Leatherwood Creek with a specified number of concerts to be held each summer.

Luckily, extra federal funds became available in 1937 and there were 2,400 WPA workers in Lawrence County That was a timely coincidence which enabled city officials to carry out the terms of the gift. Bedford used many of those workers to build and develop Otis Park. The Works Project Administration provided employment and did much good work for our community. The long handled shovel was the tool of most WPA work gangs and it might take thirty men all day to dig a ditch that today's heavy machinery can dig in an hour. Thousands of feet of stone fences were built by hand.

However, workers also had the reputation of loafing on the job and there were jokes reported of men being injured by falls from leaning on their shovels until the handle broke. There was a true incident when a work gang was caught spending several hours on a funeral services for a mole they had killed; complete with a grave and cement headstone. Some said WPA stood for 'we piddle around'.

Mayor Henry 'Dot' Murray and Mr. Otis were determined to build the park and made frequent visits to their new to check on the progress of the WPA workers. Mayor Murray served until 1941 and saw that all required projects were completed, including the swimming pool, maintaining the 1865 Civil War era mansion, band shell, stone bridges and fences. Fred Otis lived until 1945 to see his family name memorialized and his gift to eastside children recognized as one of the best parks and municipal golf courses in Indiana. Dutchtown kids enjoyed the Otis Park pool on 'free days' and skinny dippin' in Big Bend in Leatherwood Creek after golfers went home.

The value of Otis Park golf course often goes unrecognized by parents and school corporations who have benefitted most of all. Few small communities have the benefit of such a facility to provide thousands of hours of recreation and team sports for adults and youngsters down through the years. Thousands of boys and girls have excelled in golf, our High School teams rank high in the state and several graduates have become golf professionals, including Doc and his brother.

Otis Park golf course is one the best municipal courses in Southern Indiana and it attracts golfers from miles away to come and challenge its hills, valleys and greens. It is a great asset for our community as a tourist attraction. Local motels would do well to promote 'golf vacation packages'. I have benefitted from Otis Park as a swimmer, caddy and golfer since the day it was established in 1935, except that time I worked a few years for Uncle Sam.

The generous gift of Fred B. Otis has been a blessing to the people of Bedford for eighty-one years and will continue into the future as a true example of one man's citizenship and community service.

Caddy Shack

One day, some of the older guys told us about caddying and four of us decided to go out and ask for a job. I had caddied once when Dad arranged my first job to caddy for County Clerk, Ruel Steele. The Caddy master put Chad, Doc, Tuffy and I on the caddy list and the golf course became our best source of income. Skinny decided to keep his paper route and practice basketball. The new job came just in time for a new bike and Dad took me to the Goodyear Store. The red and white balloon tired bike had a price tag of $29.95. Dad made the $ 5.00 down payment, and said it was up to me to earn the $1.25 weekly payments. It was my first Economics lesson and just like that, I was up to my ears in debt, but I was mobile. No more 'shanks mare' for me, I rode to the golf course, school, family errands and taught my dog Zero to ride in the basket on the handlebars. I rode that bike for six years and handed it down to my sister and brother.

Golfers insisted on a well disciplined caddy system to prevent caddies rushing out to hassle them for a job as soon as they pulled into the parking lot. We were required to stay down in the brand new Caddy Shack, a limestone building with a matching outhouse clinging to the side of the bluff across the road from number one tee. Pro Shop restrooms were off- limits to caddies.

160

The Caddy Master kept the operation running smoothly. His job was to supervise 40 or 50 caddies, keep the golfers happy and see that all caddies got to earn a little spending money. He kept a daily sign-in sheet in his basement work area under the pro-shop to determine when we would be called up to the 'promised land' to carry a golf bag. We got to the course early in the morning on days we wanted to work. The list was not the final word, because many golfers had regular caddies or insisted on older kids or men.

Caddying allowed us to earn money all summer, but they put young kids at the bottom of the pecking order at the caddy shack and we got the duffers and low tippers. Otis caddies were ranked in three classes: Class A, men and top-notch caddies earned seventy cents for eighteen holes; Class B got sixty cents; Class C was reserved for skinny beginners; we were paid four bits (half dollar.) We were at the bottom of the salary schedule but more than happy to carry some old duffer's clubs 18 holes at those slave labor wages. Golf carts were years in the future and walking an eighteen hole round took five or more hours. Golfers walked the course while caddies carried the golf bags and kept track of their golf balls. Some golfers gave a small tip, but that vanished if you lost a ball in the rough. Caddies could also earn cash by 'shagging' for golfers wanting to practice their game. Otis didn't have a driving range, only a practice area between today's two practice greens. Golfers brought their own bag of practice balls and the caddy stood out in the fairway with the empty bag to pick up (shag) balls hit at him. Good eyesight was a definite asset for the job.

There was no 'dress code' for caddies, we rarely wore shirts and some guys were barefoot. We were treated as minorities on days we worked and had to stay in the caddy shack area. We experienced discrimination as the 'untouchables' and required to stay in the shadows until we were called up. Caddies were not allowed inside the Pro Shop, but we could visit the Pro Shop concessions window to buy drinks or candy bars. My usual fifteen cent lunch was a cold bottle of RC Cola and a box of Cheezits. The caddy shack was a dark and dingy lunchroom, so many sunny days we sneaked down to the WPA rock garden for lunch to enjoy the flowers and waterfalls Mr. Otis had specified in his gift. Then, it was back to the caddy shack to wait and hope our name would be called. I got better jobs as I got older, and by the age of sixteen I would often carry two bags and double my income. Most hot days after the golfers went home, we went 'skinny dipping' in Big Bend swimming hole where Leatherwood Creek crosses the present seventeenth fairway. (see cover)

Crowds of kids our age used the swimming pool, ate and played the jukebox in pro-shop area, but caddies were banned to the Caddy Shack. It was tough on the ego, but you followed the rules if you wanted to work The Otis Park pool had two great attractions, it was cleaner than the creek and it was where girls sunbathed and watched boys show off on the diving boards. Naturally, Chad, Doc, Tuffy and I took a day off once in a while, managed to find swimming suits and joined the crowd. Tuesday and Thursday were slow days so we used some of our caddy money to swim in the pool. Both city pools had low and high diving boards in those days and we could show off our diving skills for the girls.

One summer the new golf pro hired me and Doc to help his teenage nephew work at the sandwich and drinks concession counter in the clubhouse. He only paid us a dollar a day for about five hours work. However, he said we could have free hamburgers and cokes. He fired us after two months because we were eating up his profits! I really enjoyed that time out of the caddy shack because I got to sell food and cokes to all my classmates using the swimming pool, and feeding nickels to the big Wurlitzer juke box.

Friday was Caddy Day, but only in the morning, and we got to play golf free, so we scrounged for used clubs. Chad and I found a set hanging in the office at Rainey's junkyard, and bought it for five dollars. The warped hickory shafts, rusty iron blades and chipped heads on the woods didn't bother our skills; we had none. Lucky Doc got an old set from his Grandpa and we started playing golf seventy- nine years ago. We played every Friday morning and sometimes late in the evening. I recall moonlit nights when we used a lighted cigarette to mark the hole for putting practice.

Doc and I made the Bedford High golf team and after the war, Doc joined the list of several Bedford kids who have become Golf Professionals. I'm still trying to master the game, but once in a while, I shoot my age. It's easier when you're ninety-one!

Most caddies served in World War II and sadly most have passed, but when I meet an oldtimer, we talk about the 'good old depression days' and stretch our memories to recall the names of boys who caddied with us at Otis Park. Of course we always recall those older caddies who tossed us into the creek on days when things got boring! Leatherwood Creek flows below the present parking lot and a small dam gave hikers a limestone walkway across the creek and formed a pretty pool of water about three feet deep. It was a perfect place to toss a kid into the creek and there was a worn path down the bluff used by the big guys who took us down to 'baptize us' in the cool water!

One grabbed your feet, the other your hands and stretched you out like a sack of sand. They would swing you back and forth a couple of times and on the count of three, you went flying out into the water. Some hot days, Doc and I took the positive side of the event; we couldn't fight the big guys so we just ran down and jumped in. It was a great way to save your dignity and cool off on a hot summer day. Looking back eighty years, I remember that the Otis park Caddy Shack money paid for my bike, school clothes and Saturday night movies. I am sure the strict discipline and treatment we endured made the teens of the Great Depression better equipped to accept rules and follow orders in the Armed Services a few years later.

Today, the dam is gone, the swimming pool is a parking lot, the dilapidated caddy shack is empty. Only the Pool House has been saved.

The days when a skinny kid was glad to carry a golfbag eighteen holes for fifty cents has passed, but wouldn't those old boys be amazed to learn golfers now pay over fifty cents a hole to cruise the course in gas powered golf carts!

Watermelon Feast

We were skinny dippin' in the cool waters of Big Bend one hot August day when Tuffy announced that he had a secret we would all like. He had our instant attention and we were all ears to learn what he had up his sleeve. It was really good news, our gang had been invited to enjoy a free watermelon feast! Watermelons were a summer treat enjoyed by any kid who could get his hands on one and every red-blooded Dutchtown kid carried a pocket knife in case a free melon crossed his path. Tuffy went on to explain our good fortune,

"My cousin, Hank lives on a farm about five miles out on the Tunnelton Road and his Dad raises watermelons. Hank said he would chill two or three ripe melons in the cool water of the Springhouse if we wanted to come out to the farm sometime before school starts."

Labor Day was creeping up on us and we didn't have much vacation time left, so we decided the next Tuesday would be a good day to stuff ourselves with cool watermelon. Tuffy said he would see Hank at church Sunday and make sure that would be okay for us to come out. Skinny couldn't go because he might not get back in time for of basketball practice. The rest of us decided to ride our bikes to Otis, 'sign in' to keep our names on the caddy list and then ride to Hank's farm.

Tuesday was a beautiful morning for a bike ride, we stopped at the golf course just long enough to sign in and were back on the blacktop. Our bicycles were nothing like the modern muti-geared, thin tired speedy racers. They were heavy iron framed monsters with balloon tires and only one speed; slow. Pumping those pedals was tough work and we were panting and ready to take a break at the roadside spring by the old quarry before but we got to the airport. A tin cup was hanging on a post so we drank, soused our heads with cold spring water and rested a while. The road leveled out along the airport and we pedaled easier and faster. A mile or so later we coasted down the long hill to Duncan's

Bend and across the Guthrie Creek Bridge. Tuffy said we were almost to Hank's farm, and our day got brighter as we followed our leader and pumped madly on with visions of ripe red watermelon waiting at Hank's farm in the sandy soil of the White River bottoms.

We passed several farmhouses with big watermelon patches before Tuffy finally stopped at a sandy driveway marked only by a rusty mail box nailed to a tree. He proudly announced that we had reached our goal, but Chad, Doc and I were hot, thirsty and puzzled because there was no farmhouse in sight. Chad yelled at him,

"What do you mean, we're here, what are you talking about, where's the farm? I'm tired and thirsty, I wan'ta see cold watermelons"!

Tuffy got mad and fired back,

"Okay, Okay, keep your shirt on. Hank's house is a ways off the road down this sandy lane. We'll be sinking our teeth into watermelon in no time."

We followed him down the lane but pumping a heavy bicycle through loose sand was nearly impossible and pushing it was almost as bad. Finally, we left them on the side of the lane and 'hoofed it' the rest of the way. We stopped at the yard gate of a very quiet farmhouse with a bunch of squawking chickens in the henhouse. Tuffy yelled out for Hank, but didn't get an answer. He yelled louder two more times and Hank didn't answer, but Doc did,

"Hey Tuffy, Hank's not here, there's nobody home! Do you see a car or truck in sight? Give it up. They're gone so let' git a drink from that pump in the yard and git over in the shade to rest. Maybe they'll come back after while."

We were in the yard pumping up water when a big woman with a bloody apron and carrying an axe came from the back of the house! Three of us cleared the yard in record time, but Tuffy stood his ground and said,

"Hi Aunt Mary, it's me, Tuffy. Where's Hank? He invited us to come out today for a watermelon feast."

I felt a lot better when she put down that bloody axe, smiled and began talking to Tuffy,

"Sorry I didn't git out here sooner, Tuffy, but I wuz out in the back killing a chicken for supper and didn't hear you. I'm so sorry I couldn't tell you boys he couldn't do it today, but we don't have a phone. Hank had to help his Dad haul a load of watermelons to a grocery store in Mitchell today and we don't have a ripe watermelon on the place Well, we all understood her excuse, because none of us had phones, either. However, that part about 'no ripe watermelons' nearly broke our hearts. I guess she saw how disappointed we were because her next idea sounded like a pretty good alternative.

"Hey, Tuffy, we may not have watermelon, but we've got corn, I can boil up a mess of roasting ears real fast fur you boys".

We enjoyed the roasting ears and rested a while before taking long swigs from the pump. Aunt Mary gave Tuffy a Mason jar full of water to get us back to the spring by the airport. We plodded back down the lane to our bikes and pushed them through the sand back to the road. Chad took the lead and we pedaled past a couple of melon patches before he stopped at one and said,

"Boys, we've been looking all day for a watermelon, now there's a field full of 'em and I think we ought'a git one!"

We were hot and frustrated and we all had bicycle baskets, but we agreed to take only one, why would the farmer miss just one watermelon? Chad climbed the fence, thumped two or three to be sure he got a ripe one before handing over a nice stripped one for Doc to put in my bike basket.

We thought no one was watching, but just then I saw a little old lady come out of a house way down the road, She yelled, jumped in her car and tore down the road past us like a bat out of Hell. Doc said,

"Uh oh, she sure gave us a dirty look as she whizzed past, I think we're in big trouble. We better git outta' here pronto."

We pedaled fast but I was last. I was handicapped by the heavy melon rolling around in my bike basket. Our goal was to get past the all houses and across the road, but we never made it. A posse of two mad women, one short one tall, cut us off at the pass. They were waiting by the side of the road at the next house and were armed with brooms. I thought it was appropriate because they looked like witches. The tall one was evidently the farm owner and the little one was the speedy squealer who nearly ran over us. We knew the jig was up so we pulled over and stopped. I had the melon but Chad decided to do the talking. He tried the 'polite and playing-on-their -sympathy' approach.

"We're sorry Ma'am and we'll give back the melon. You had so many and we only took one. We thought you wouldn't mind if we picked just one. You look like a good Christian.

The tall woman said,

"Nice try sonny, but you boys are just sorry you got caught! Now hand over my watermelon and git on down the road before I call the Sherriff."

Well, it was obvious that his plea had fallen on mad, deaf ears, so I lifted the melon out my bike basket and said,

"Okay, here, take your precious melon. We didn't hurt it and we didn't plug it, so we don't even know if it's ripe."

The old witch took the melon and I saw a glint in her eyes before she threw us her final insult,

"Oh, you didn't know whether it was ripe or not, eh! Well let's find out!"

She hoisted our melon over her head and smashed it the blacktop road. Green rind, bright red melon and black seeds flew in all directions. That was the only ripe watermelon we had seen all day. I'm sure the old lady thought she had won, but I think maybe we won when Tuffy said,

"So long you old Stingy Gut, I'll bet they won't let you in church next Sunday."

We pedaled away in a hurry and it was a long road back to town. The next day we told Skinny about our 'wild goose chase' and he had a good laugh at our expense before he asked,

"Why didn't you just lie and say you meant to pay for it"?

My answer was simple,

"We were caught rustling a watermelon and remember: Straight Shooters always win --- Law Breakers always lose!"

Years later I asked Tuffy if he remembered the time we got caught stealing that watermelon. He was quick to answer:

"Yeah, we got busted, but so did the watermelon!"

Quarry Swimming

It was another muggy August day at Otis Park Golf Course; too hot for golfers so there were no caddying jobs. It was also too hot to stay in the Caddy Shack, so we sneaked down the bluff behind it, along the creek and up into the into the Rock Garden (forbidden territory for caddies.) We sprawled out in the grass under the deep shade of the Maple trees and relaxed. On such a hot day, the rock garden was an oasis with a cool breeze, fish ponds and miniature waterfalls. However, the peace and quiet was broken by the honking horn of a rattletrap car. Joe Stone and his Model A Ford had arrived upon the scene and he yelled,

"Hey, who wants to go swimmin' at Swingin' Bridge in Oolitic?"

Joe was a high school graduate with a part time job. In other words, he was a man of means, who only caddied on his time off. He had scrapped and saved to buy a old jalopy with way too many miles, but it was his pride and joy. He had become a pretty good 'shade tree mechanic' and he kept the tired little four cylander motor purring like a kitten.

Quarry swimming was an interesting thought, but there was a catch to the invitation. Joe was willing to drive us to Oolitic to enjoy the clear blue waters of the Swinging Bridge quarry hole, if we paid for the gas! Now, money was hard to come by in those days and gas cost thirteen cents a gallon. Several guys said they were not good swimmers and others decided to wait in case golfers came out later in the day.

Chad took the practical solution and said,

"Heck, let's just walk up the creek and swim in Big Bend."

Skinny reminded him, "Yes, but the golf pro said 'no skinny dippin,' if you wanna caddy.' So, let's take a ride with Joe."

I had never been to Swinging Bridge, but I had a spare dime and was ready to go. Five of us chipped in enough cash to buy gas for the adventure and piled into the old Ford. Our chauffer took the back roads out past Dive school, down through Breckenridge and East Oolitic. He admitted he was avoiding the main roads because his license plates weren't up to date! After a winding ride through the back country, we reached the Swinging Bridge limestone quarry on Highway 37 (old 37) just north of Oolitic. Joe pulled off the road to park and we walked less than fifty feet to peer down into a large deserted stone quarry hole full of sparkling sky blue water. It was absolutely the largest 'blue hole quarry' I had ever seen! However, there was a problem; we were standing on a ledge thirty feet above the water. There were only two ways down; walk across the rickety 'swinging bridge' to a pile of rocks or go down a tall ladder. We chose the ladder and carefully climbed down to the quarry floor about three feet above the blue water. Some said it was about thirty feet deep! It was our great private pool and we stripped for skinny dippin' There was an escape ladder fastened to the wall to enter or climb out of the water but Joe said the usual routine was to dive from the three foot ledge, swim about thirty feet to crawl out on a stack of stone to sun, swim or dive. The deep quarry water was very cold but we could stretch out on a hot block of limestone to sun bath a while. Nobody dared to swim too far away from the only ways out of the water. The sun beamed down on our skinny naked bodies and swimming in the cool blue waters of the big deserted quarry was a tropical treat that afternoon. Our teenage interest in girls had peaked and someone started telling Doofus jokes on the trip back to Otis Park. I remember, Joe told the one that topped all others.

"One afternoon, Doofus took his girl friend for a ride in his Model A. They were driving down to the crossroads General Store for a coke. Half way there he had to shift gears and his hand slipped off the stick shift knob onto her knee! She giggled and said he could go a little farther if he wanted to – so he drove her all the way to town."

Joe dropped us off at the rock garden and we told him the gas money had been worth the trip. We made several more excursions to Swinging Bridge that summer before Joe figured he would get drafted, so he enlisted in the Army to get a steady job.

Our area had many 'blue holes' on the edge of town, but Swinging Bridge was the largest. Quarry swimming was free and you didn't need a swimsuit. However, it was dangerous recreation and several swimmers drowned in the cold water, due to cramps, dare-devil challenges like diving off ledges or distance races. Some deaths were due to the limited ways out of a quarry hole because of the steep stone walls.

I stopped quarry swimming when one of my high school buddies drowned during the summer of our junior year in 1942. Swimming in creeks, ponds or rivers was safer, because you could wade out! Of course, the city pools were safest, but they cost money; besides most of us didn't own a swimming suit! That day in 1939, our private pool was a giant limestone quarry, idled by the stock market crash of 1929! The quarry machinery stood silent among giant stacks of limestone and there were no quarry workers. Stone from Swinging Bridge was used in the Empire State building, federal buildings state capitols, mansions and across the United States. Hundreds of worker quarried out the top quality Indiana limestone to be shipped across the United States for state, federal and commercial buildings still in use. Limestone is one of the most durable building materials and there were more than thirty quarries and stone mills operating in Lawrence County before the Great Depression squelched the demand. Unemployment sky- rocketed to twenty-four percent and many quarry workers and stone carvers left town. The empty quarries and stone mills across stood idle until after World War II. Today, the stone business is doing well and most of the 'blue holes' have been drained or filled in with stone.

Quarry swimming is a dangerous memory reserved for members of the World War II generation.

Happy Days

Leaving Lincoln for grades seven and eight in the Bedford Junior High school was a real psychological jolt. We had to leave our neighborhood school and cross the tracks into unfamiliar territory. It was a walk of about seven blocks across town to an ancient three-story brick Junior High School. We faced a new daily class schedule of home rooms, study halls, and changing rooms and teachers for each subject. Gone was our classroom with one teacher all day. School promotions were not 'social promotions' in those days and if you failed a grade, you repeated it. Junior High was the point where many over- age boys quit school. Our buddy Ernie made that decision the day he turned sixteen.

The Junior High School and High School were located in the same block with the basketball gym and it was the hub of athletic activity. Our Phys Ed classes were basketball and running. Skinny was as happy as a rabbit in a briar patch when he made the seventh grade team. Basketball was king in Southern Indiana and the gyms were full on game nights and there was not a football team in the area. Bedford was recognized state-wide for strong basketball teams and Lawrence County had ten high schools. We held our own sectional tournament each March and there was intense rivalry among the schools and basketball stars and coaches were considered local heroes. Outstanding teams from Mitchell and Bedford both had reached the Indiana State Finals by 1943 and many Lawrence County boys went on to play college basketball.

My eighth grade English teacher was a customer on my paper route and I was very careful to toss her paper on the porch However, in mid-winter she organized debating teams as a class project and my average student partner and I were paired against the two top students to debate the question, 'Is it better to live in the country or the city.' We argued for the country life and were soundly defeated and humiliated in front of the class. I'm ashamed to report that old lady's paper missed her porch several times that winter. One of my opponents was Claude Akins, who went into acting after the war and a stint at Indiana University and Northwestern. He became a movie and television star and character actor and had many important roles in movies, especially Westerns. He did three television series including a long run of Sheriff Lobo. I didn't feel too badly losing to Claude because he was a regular guy. One WPA project was a sewing shop to hire women to make clothing for school children. I was embarrassed by the W.P.A. sewing shop jacket I wore in Jr. High, but he said it looked fine. He attended some of our Bedford High School class reunions, and we played a round of golf at Otis in an annual Golf Tourney named in his honor to raise funds to improve our parks. Claude was still a down-home guy with that big smile he used so often in his acting career.

Bedford High School was loaded with teachers who were intent on making scholars of all of us. I enjoyed the freshman year with all the new teachers and classes. Lunch in high school, like my prior schools, was Sloppy Joes sandwiches, soup and milk. I could have chili, a Sloppy Joe and a pint of milk for two bits, but then I found out the Jones Grocery Store across the street (now the Shell station} also sold lunch. The 'Mom and Pop' enterprise had fixed up a back room with benches around a pot-bellied stove. We could buy two doughnuts and a pint of chocolate milk for twelve cents. For entertainment, we could go down on the alley to smoke or feed the milk goats in the Jones barn. On top of all those benefits, I had a little free time and an extra thirteen cents to put in my pocket every day the weather cooperated. So guess where I ate lunch most days?

Hoover's Confectionary on the west side of the town square was our malt shop and a popular hang-out for teenagers. Prices were very reasonable in 1941-42, fountain cokes were five cents, sodas or shakes, fifteen cents, and Coneys were two for a quarter. Every booth had a juke box selection unit with six records for a quarter. It was a great place to meet and greet. Popular dress was boys in yellow 'senior cords' decorated with graffiti from class members and girls in pleated skirts, penny loafers and bobby socks. The crowd was really big on Friday nights after basketball games and on Saturday nights before the Midnight Movies, which started at 11:00pm. Standing on the sidewalk or loafing in a buddy's car was a good place to hang out 'watching all the girls go by'. Most of the girls in our class eventually passed by and our 'Hubba-Hubbas' and wolf whistles were endured by some girls and greatly appreciated by others!

Firpo's Drive In, a rustic drive-in with few cars, was our other teenage watering hole. It was only a block from the high school and served as our Arnold's from the television show 'Happy Days'. Those of us without cars rode bikes or walked to Firpo's with our dates. Parents were very wary of a boy with a car and Shanks Mare (walking) was the usual method of transportation. I met my wife, June, at Hoover's after the war.

The Saturday Midnight Show was the biggest event of the week for teenage dating, waiting in a long ticket line was half the fun and the balcony was full of couples who never saw the movie. Of course, many parents worried about their daughter walking home with a date at one o'clock in the morning.

Walking your date home was a very pleasant experience especially, on a dark night when you were in dark spots between the street lights!

War Clouds

The world changed quickly in 1938 and war news filled most of the Movietone news reels at the theaters. Hitler stripped all German Jews off their Civil Rights and ordered they wear the yellow Star of David on their clothing for identification. He was building his Third Reich, Mussolini was in power in Italy, and Japan was ravaging the Far East. News reels at the movies reported it, but we laughed at the 'goose stepping' German troops marching into conquered countries. The war news grew worse every week, but our country was struggling to come out of the depression and our leaders were busy looking the other way. The guys in our gang needed to earn money to pay for bikes, clothes and movies. High School was at hand and the war was too far away to worry us.

Inflation had not yet raised its ugly head in 1940 and the Cost of Living figures were low, but money was scarce and living was hard! The minimum wage was thirty cents an hour with an average annual income of $2,059. Examples of prices Included: Loaf of bread .08 -- Gallon of milk .34 --- Dozen eggs .16

New car--- $995 --- Gallon of gas .19 --- House $6,954 --- Postage stamp--- .03

Our gang spent less time together as other interests in money, sports and girls had taken preference, but we made the long hike to school every morning to compare notes and make weekend plans. However, we spent many of those days in a in a new location on Leatherwood Creek. Caddying at Otis Park drew us away from fishing and swimming at Sycamore and Clay Banks and we drifted upstream to Big Bend, a deep hole on the golf course. The money was at the golf course, the girls were at the swimming pool and the dogs were left home.

Leatherwood Creek flows into the golf course under a limestone bridge course, meets a stone bluff and bends at a right angle for a new route down the valley below the Caddy Shack. It continues under a second Fred Otis bridge, flows behind his Band Shell through Dutchtown territory and on to White River. Our new swimming hole was Big Bend which was created at that big turn. It was wide, deep and just a few yards up the creek from the Caddy Shack. We could skinny dip until we got called up to caddy and it was a perfect spot to wash off the sweat after caddying four hours. Skinny dippin' was okay as long as we stayed in the water when golfers were in the area. In fact, we earned extra money diving for golf balls and selling them to passing golfers. We were sort of Hoosier pearl divers until a new Golf Pro banned swimming and put an end to our income because he also sold golf balls! Caddies hunted the course for lost balls and usually observed the unwritten rule that a ball is not 'lost' until it stops rolling. Golf was an expensive sport in the Depression and we made extra money selling golf balls. Most caddies had regular customers in town who would buy used balls. Some wanted only the new Red Dot Acushnet balls.

Big bend was about six foot deep with enough room to share it with the usual occupants of fish, frogs, turtles and water snakes. One July day it was so hot and muggy in the caddy Shank that we were scooted down the bluff to go up to Big Bend for a swim and saw Mose fishing for bass. It was really great to see him again and we visited a while before going on up the creek. A surprise was waiting on the banks of Big Bend. Chad was leading and he found a big snake sunning on a flat rock near three golf balls. Chad thought it was a water snake and started to kick it out of the way to get the balls when Skinny yelled,

"Look out Chad! It's a copperhead, don't let it git in the crick!"

We managed to keep it surrounded until Skinny found a club and vigorously beat it to death. Chad got mad and argued that it was not a copperhead. Tuffy and Doc sided with him and they began yelling at Skinny for killing a harmless water snake. I figured Skinny was right because it looked just like those copperheads we saw in the Cement Plant cabin. None of us were experts on snakes because our dogs usually chased them away before we saw them. The argument got pretty loud but was quickly settled when Mose came up the creek behind us and yelled one loud question.

"Hey guys, who killed this big copperhead?"

Jobs and Finances

Caddy fees had increased seventy cents a round, but winter put an end to caddying and I got a Saturday job in one of the three shoe repair shops in town. Shoe repair was a good business because people couldn't afford new shoes so they would have the cobbler replace their soles and heels. My sophomore year there was a National Youth Corps program in High School and needy students could work twenty-four hours a month and earn $6.00. I thought two bits an hour was okay for staying after school and helping a history teacher I really liked. Another job was guarding the bicycle racks at noon with Spencer Flynn, a senior who joined the Eighth Air Corps after graduation. (He died in a B-17 mid-air collision over England a year before I arrived.}

Hunters roamed the woods to trap foxes or raccoons for skins to sell to a fur- buyer who set up his 'trading post' on the town square on Saturday mornings. Trapping was another way to get skins so Chad and I decided we should run a trap line to make some extra money. We had seen several muskrats on Leatherwood Creek while we caddied during the summer, so we invested a few dollars in used steel traps to get rich. Muskrat trapping involved several steps; find the den and muskrat slide on the bank of the creek, set an open the trap in the water beneath the slide and anchor the trap chain to a stake on the bank. We set all our traps and were up at dawn on those cold winter days to run our trap line before school and on weekends. Snow and icy water was part of the muskrat trapping business, but our optimism waned after a few weeks. Both of us had colds and our catch was only one unlucky muskrat. We suspended operations, skinned our catch, put the pelt on a stretch-board and waited for it to cure. The fur buyer gave us four bits (fifty cents) for that skin. We divided the money, sold our steel traps and retired from the trapping business.

I hit the big money at age sixteen, just in time to buy my eleven dollar class ring. I got hired at Bill's Auto store on the town square and worked two hours after school and thirteen hours on Saturday (8:00 am to 9:00 pm) for six bucks a week. They hired Tuffy a few weeks later and we took care of the service area. Basically, we were battery and tire changers, but clerks when needed. Cars were not too complicated in those days and many men did their own repairs and there were many small repair shops scattered around the county. Bill's Auto sold most of the parts, needed by these shade tree mechanics. I never really mastered all the manuals for generators, starters, piston rings, mufflers and tailpipes, I concentrated on spark plugs, batteries, tire boots and decorative accessories like seat covers, steering wheel knobs and mud flaps. There were several Bill's Auto Stores in Louisville and southern Indiana and the big city sales manager made a monthly visit to boost sales. We dreaded his visits because always had 'big city' ideas to boost sales. One technique we considered dangerous was when he would step out on the sidewalk, grab the arm of a prospective customer, pull him into the store and demonstrate a piece of equipment. We were afraid some 'big old boy' might kill him! We paid close attention until he left, but not one of us ever tried that method of selling in Bedford.

Setting pins at the Model Bowling alley became a source of income during my Senior year. There were no automatic pin-setting machines and we had to reset the pins manually with a special rack. We had to jump into the pit each time the bowler rolled the ball, grab the knocked down pins and put them in the rack. We had to lift the ball up into the return gutter to send it back to the bowler for a second try, pull down the pin rack and hop up out of the pit before the next bowler rolled the ball. We picked up pins every time a ball came thundering down the alley and bowlers expected us to be really fast in league tourneys. Chad and I could set two alleys at a time, and earn the magnificent sum of ten cents a game for each bowler. On League nights, with five men on a team, we could make good money setting double. Leagues bowled three games so we could earn a six dollar night! My senior year I worked at Bill's Auto store from 4:00pm to 6:00 pm, ate a snack and walked across the square to set pins from 7:00 pm until 10:00 pm.

I endured various experiences of 'doing without' right up to the day I got may draft notice. I was a six foot teenager who weighed 150 pounds soaking wet. Obesity was not a problem in the Depression generation, food was scarce and folks lived without the fattening fast food hamburgers and high fructose sodas served kids today. Our idea of 'fast food' was rabbits or squirrels. As a teenager, I earned spending money with several part-time jobs which no longer exist. I could caddy at the golf course, set pins at the bowling alley, get a newspapers route or work at Bill's Auto Store until the start of WW II. Times were tough; I did all three and never earned more than twenty-five cents an hour!

Pearl Harbor - the War at Home

Sunday, December 7, 1941 the Empire of Japan made a sneak attack on Pearl Harbor while their envoys were in Washington discussing peace. The bombing ended all thought of isolation and propelled us into World War II. I remember the family sitting around the old Atwater-Kent radio to hear President Roosevelt's war speech to Congress after Pearl Harbor.

"Yesterday, December 7, 1941---a date which will live in infamy---the United States of America was suddenly and deliberately attacked by naval and air forces of the Empire of Japan...."

Later he said the United States must become 'the Arsenal of Democracy'. Perhaps Japan's attack on Pearl Harbor did us a favor. It awakened our nation and we declared war on the three Axis countries who intended to rule the world. We also rounded up thousands of Japanese in this country and put them in camps because we feared sabotage. The USA had stood by and watched Germany and Italy conquer Europe and North Africa. We were in the Great depression and not ready for war and Germany was attacking England in the 'Battle of Britain'

Pearl Harbor was a shock and we talked about it walking to Bedford High Monday morning but had no idea how greatly that sneak attack would change our lives. The bombing of Pearl Harbor found our nation in the Depression and unprepared for war but unemployment dropped from twenty-four percent to zero as able-bodied men went to war and women went to work in defense work to produce enough tanks, ships, and planes to fight and win a war in both Europe and the Pacific. 'Remember Pearl Harbor' became our battle cry as millions of men and women enlisted or were called for service. Thousands of teenagers joined the military or were drafted and often, two or more members from a family were called to serve.

The nation's sense of security was so badly shaken that the government forced Japanese families living in California into internment camps as a precaution against sabotage. Air-raid watch and warning systems used volunteers as Air-raid Wardens to search the skies for enemy bombers. Black-out drills and air-raid drills were practiced in schools. One summer night in 1943, Chad and Doc and I sat on a hill at Otis Park and watched the entire town go dark as the air-raid siren screamed for a practice blackout. We didn't realize that we would soon hear real air raid warnings in combat zones. Civilian life changed drastically and the war effort had first priority on all materials. Rationing coupons were issued in late 1942 and coupon books of stamps for gasoline, tires, sugar, meat and coffee became a fact of life. Gas ration cards of class 'A' allowed the driver only three gallons per week. There was a 'B' card for farmers and workers driving to defense plants

The shortage of tires and inter-tubes was a huge problem which limited travel. Hoarding tires was illegal, and motorists could only own five tires per car. Priorities were given to doctors and essential workers. A permit from the County Ration Board was needed to purchase a new tire. I was working at Bill's Auto Store, and we sold hundreds of tire inter-tube repair kits containing glue and rubber patches. There were also heavy patches (boots) to glue inside worn out tires to cover holes and get a few more miles and a bumpy ride out a worn out tire with very little tread.

Our nation's auto industry concentrated on building jeeps, trucks and tanks for our troops. No new cars were manufactured in for civilians 1942 through 1944 and people relied on repair parts and 'shade tree mechanics' to keep their cars on the road. Speed limits were lowered to

34 mph and carpools were encouraged to save gas and tires. This wasn't a drastic change, as many cars in those days couldn't go much faster.

Millions went to work in factories at $1.35 per hour to produce planes, tanks, and ships needed for victory. A large percentage of the aircraft workers were women who did the riveting on approximately 230,000 airplanes building. Norman Rockwell's famous painting of 'Rosie the Riveter', a muscular beauty wearing work clothes, a red bandana and holding a riveting gun appeared on the cover of the Saturday Evening Post. Rosie became the symbol of women working to build the Arsenal of Democracy. The original painting sold for 4.9 million dollars at an auction in May, 2002. Nationwide, thousands of women were employed in dangerous jobs in munitions plants. 'Praise the Lord and Pass the Ammunition' became a popular war-time song. There were War Bond drives, and schools encouraged children to bring in loose change to purchase War Stamps.

Defense plants in my home state of Indiana produced B-17 engines at the Studebaker factory in South Bend. The Allison Division of General Motors in Indianapolis made several thousand fighter engines. Evansville's Chrysler facility produced millions of .45 caliber bullets. Aircraft wings for the P-47 Thunderbolts were also made in Evansville by an appliance factory. Most importantly, an Indianapolis plant secretly produced 14,000 of the top-secret Norden bombsights. Locally, the Milwaukee railroad hauled defense workers twenty-five miles to the assembly lines at the new Crane Naval Ammunition Depot. This large Naval Depot was constructed in 1940 in a large area west of Bedford for the production and storage of shells and bombs was in full production. High School teenagers over sixteen and college students were hired to work on weekends. A large Army smokeless powder plant at Charlestown was constructed in conjunction with Burns City (Crane) storage depot. It employed many men and women from Lawrence County. They sometimes slept in cars or tents to avoid the daily 120 mile round trip and save time, gasoline and tires. Special gas ration cards were available for defense workers in carpools. It was easy to identify Charlestown workers, because all had yellow hands from preparing powder charges for artillery shells. Doc said his Dad used a lot of soap, but couldn't get it off. Several area idle stone mill buildings were converted into defense factories making parts for tanks and aircraft engine parts. A number of high school boys became welders and worked nights until they entered the armed services.

The Draft - Congress passed the Selective Service and Training Act in September of 1940 as war clouds gathered in Europe and the Pacific area. The first peacetime draft for military service required all men ages 21 to 35 to register with local Draft Boards. Teenagers were added after Pearl Harbor and were required to register and be classified as:

1 A ---- healthy single men
3 A ---- man with wife and children
3 D -----extreme hardship to family
4 F ---- those physically or mentally unfit
4 A ---- too old
2 B --- workers in war industry plants
2 C --- farmers, agricultural workers1
A-O Conscientious objector limited to non- military service

A lottery system was used to draw names of the draftees and nobody wanted to win that one. That '4 F plague' hit the neighborhood quickly and other guys developed a weak heart or other serious ailments. We said they just didn't have the heart to go! Others suddenly became very religious and claimed to be 'conscientious objectors' who didn't believe in fighting for their country. Millions of young people volunteered to serve, but theawr was a terrible experience for parents who had struggled to feed and protect their children during the hunger and tribulations' of the world's greatest Depression. They had high hopes for a better future for their children, only to have them jerked away and sent to war. Young families were destroyed when fathers were forced to leave a wife and children to serve their country. The war touched everyone and a majority of Dutchtown families were affected by so many young men going off to military service. A six by ten inch Blue Star banner was designed for families with a husband, son or daughter in the Armed Forces The small red banners with a blue star in a white center were hung in windows to show they had someone in the military. Many families had two or more stars. Newspaper headlines reported the casualties of war and the deaths of those we knew was heartbreaking.

The War Department used Western Union telegrams to notify families of the death or missing in action (MIA) of a loved one. Those sad telegrams were delivered by taxi to thousands of homes as military casualties increased. People held their breath and prayed when one drove through neighborhood. Church membership soared as families sought the help and guidance of God and prayed for the safety and life of their loved ones.

A woman of the Greatest Generation told a story of one aspect of civilian life during the war. She said,

"We lived in a small town and our two sons were in the Army. Like us, most people in our neighborhood had family members in service. Husbands, fathers and teenagers had joined or been drafted into the military. Many parents had signed letters of permission papers for teenage sons to enlist before being drafted so they could choose the branch of service they wanted.

War Department telegrams of tragic news were delivered day or night. Our local Western Union office delivery car was a black 1939 Ford. Everyone dreaded to see it driving through the neighborhood. I was scared to death every time I saw that black car and I prayed it would pass by our house. Yet, I felt guilty knowing someone else's son had died."

She said the car reminded her of a buzzard circling to find the right house to deliver the terrible news of another serviceman's death or wound. The dreaded War Telegrams kept coming and sadly more blue stars were replaced by gold stars as young men died or were MIA (missing in action) serving our country.

"Their golden youth blots out the sky, they let the comets plod. As each one flies to live or die for country and for God." ----- *Grantland Rice*

Dirty Foot Jones

Dirty Foot Jones was the terror of our 1937 sixth grade class. He was a sixth grader who had failed a grade or two and his primary goal was to get old enough to quit school. Many of his victims thought the principal should grant that wish. We all agreed that life would be much easier without his presence. I suspect that our teacher felt the same way about Ernie Jones, no middle name, just Ernie Jones. We called him by his first name, but we had several others for him! He joined our class late in the fall semester and really didn't fit in, because he was bigger and older. However, as fate would have it, he was my next door neighbor. Mom said that his parents had dumped him off with his grandparents and left town! My parents played euchre with his grandparents every Thursday night. So I was expected to be Ernie's first friend. Actually I was his first victim! His idea of fun was rough-house wrestling, which usually ended with my arm twisted behind my back until I yelled "Uncle!" He also enjoyed Indian arm wrestling and trading shoulder punches. I came to hate those Thursday night euchre sessions and my 'playtime' with Ernie!

Ernie was a guy who needed friends. He just didn't know how to adjust to this new family and school. He was mad at the world and had decided to take it out on his classmates. We had never had a class bully, but after a few weeks of punishment, we decided we would return the favor. The battle was on, but like Pogo said years later:

"We has met the enemy and he is us!"

We were too small to fight toe-to-toe with Ernie. He had whipped two or three guys in playground fights and threatened the rest of us with all kinds of bodily harm if we crossed him. We were all afraid of him and very careful not to make him mad. Our best strategy was to avoid him. But, we discovered his weakness. Our common enemy was a slow runner and he hated to be called names! So, because of his dirty old tennis shoes, Ernie was dubbed 'Dirty Foot'. Of course no one said that to his face until we developed our plan for revenge. It was time to take him down a peg or two. Our master plan was to use the relay system on Ernie. We decided to run him ragged, even though we realized he would beat the 'stuffins' out any kid he caught. My buddy, Chad was a skinny speedster, one of the fastest runners in the sixth grade accepted the challenge. We decided to make the first test run Monday after school and Chad would be first to run and tire him out.

Our gang of five waited on the playground in full view of the teacher after school. Ernie saw us and headed our way. Chad stepped forward boldly, like David facing Goliath, and yelled,

"Hey Dirty Foot, Dirty Foot Jones, bet you can't catch me!"

Ernie was shocked by the insult and an unexpected challenge, but he recovered quickly and the race was on! We all kept our fingers crossed for Chad's safety and survival. Ernie took the bait, hook, line and sinker. Chad came in when he got tired and another brave soul, Skinny, stepped out to yell Dirty Foot! Ernie would take off after his new tormentor and we managed to run him all over the neighborhood before we scattered like quail and ran home to safety. That relay race lasted several weeks. Parents were amazed that we rushed home so quickly to do our chores. Carrying in firewood for the cookstove and filling the coal bucket sure beat being ambushed and thumped by Dirty Foot!

Ernie's classroom behavior improved greatly after his grandparents received a few notes from our teacher and the Principal. Grandpa Jones had visited school and told our teacher to use her paddle any time it was needed. He assured her that another paddling would be waiting at home. Our enemy suddenly had lots of chores to do for his grandparents. Now, we felt safe and secure on the recess playground. So, we all agreed to a 'timeout' for evenings and week-ends. The race was only for before and after school hours.

This relay racing became a game that Ernie enjoyed because, as a matter of fact, he was playing with all of us and everyone was having lots of fun. Ernie wasn't too rough with guys he captured and we were all friends. Ernie became an accepted member of the gang and we changed the rules of the chase so his captives had to be on his side. Our friendship continued on into the seventh and eighth grade. Schoolwork was difficult for Ernie and he dropped out of school the summer he was sixteen. We tried to talk him out of quitting, but he had reached his limit and he was gone. We saw him around the neighborhood from time to time, but it wasn't the same. Ernie was a working man and we lost track of him when he found a job in Indianapolis.

Our class was two months into our senior year when Ernie came back to town. He was wearing an olive drab uniform complete with

Corporal's stripes on his sleeves and bright silver gunner's wings on his chest. It was October, 1942 and Ernie had found a home in the Army. He was a member of the Army Air Corps and he looked great in his uniform and neatly polished shoes. Nobody wanted to call him 'Dirty Foot now! He had come back to Bedford on furlough to see his grandparents and friends. It was a great reunion and we threw a large party in his honor before he returned to camp. It was a time for a lot of memories of the good old days at Lincoln school, when Dirty Foot Jones chased us all over Dutchtown. Corporal Ernest Jones went back to the Air Corps and we returned to our classes at Bedford High. There were a few letters, but we eventually lost contact as he moved from post to post. The last postcard I received was from Lincoln, Nebraska. Our buddy had been assigned to Combat Air Crew training on a B-17 Flying Fortress and was waiting to move to his new base.

We were seniors nearing eighteen in May, 1943. World War II was waiting for us and we were deciding whether to wait for the draft or enlist. Our gang decided to try for the Army Air Corps. This time we would be trying to catch up with Ernie. It was late in the month when this report appeared in the newspaper:

"S/Sgt Ernest D. Jones Awarded Air Medal"

We had found Ernie! The story told us he was in the Eighth Air Corps in England. His B-17 bomber crew had completed six combat missions and earned the Air Medal on May 13, 1943. S/Sgt Ernest D. Jones, a B-17 tail gunner, had been credited with shooting down two enemy fighters. We were all glad for Ernie, but we were left with a mystery. Where did that middle initial come from? He always insisted he had no middle name. We decided there was only one answer! The middle initial was Ernie's big joke on us!

That "D" stood for Dirty Foot!

Our Turn at WW II

The guys in our gang saw the writing on the wall and realized our time to serve had arrived and now we would be chasing Dirty Foot! My four buddies had graduated and were ready to enlist and choose their branch of service as soon as we completed the 1943 school year at Bedford High. Chad and Tuffy were accepted in the Army Air Cadet Program but Doc and Skinny chose the Navy. They understood my situation and why I decided to wait to be drafted in hopes of staying in school one more semester to get six credits and graduate.

Education had been a big issue in our family since the day I entered first grade at dear Old Lincoln School in 1931. Neither of my parents had attended school beyond the eighth grade and they were determined that their three offspring would be High School graduates and get good jobs. My report card was examined carefully at the end of every grade period. The school used the two semester system in those days and it nearly broke their hearts when I had pneumonia in the second grade and failed the second semester. They were happy again when I repeated and sailed through with a straight A card. However, no one suspected how that lost semester in 1932 would affect me in my senior class of 1943.

That failure in grade two had caught up with me and it was a very short wait. My eighteenth birthday was in early June and my draft notice came in the mail the next day! I applied for an exemption for one semester, but the draft board did not see it that way and I was caught in the draft with millions of others. My waiting was over and I was going with my buddies. We had experienced the hardships of civilian life during a war for about eighteen months. The armed forces needed more young men to defend our country and now we would experience the war!

The military allowed us a week or two to settle affairs before reporting for duty. We all spent time with our family, but we managed to get together several times to laugh and recall our boyhood adventures on Leatherwood Creek. We were only eighteen but keenly aware of the dangers we faced and the poor odds against our meeting again in Dutchtown. Doc had his Dad's car one night shortly before Chad and Tuffy needed to report and we were parked in front of Hoovers checking out girls. The prospects weren't too good and time was dragging when Chad said,

"Hey guys, I gotta' a great idea! Let's go skinny dippin' in Big Bend one last time!

We agreed it was a brilliant idea and Doc drove us to Otis Park and down the fairway to the banks of the creek. It was a moonlit night, but only the hoot owls witnessed our gang of five taking a final 'skinny dip' in Big Bend!

The next few days, I said goodbye to each of my buddies as they left Bedford to report for duty and their parents hung a blue star banner in the front window to show they had a son in the service. Mom hung her banner two weeks later when I left for the Army!

Our Dutchtown gang was in the war by mid-summer of 1943 and serving our country far from our boyhood days on Leatherwood Creek.

Addendum 1

My Uncle Sam had sent me a 'present' for my eighteenth birthday, June 12, 1943. It was an invitation from the local draft board to serve my country in the armed forces. The war had been going on for a year and a half and the situation was serious. All males eighteen and over were required to register for military service! I was classified as 1 A which literally meant he's ready to go' as soon as he turns eighteen'. It was the same 'Greetings' letter sent to millions of men drafted to save our country from the Axis powers.

"Greetings:

Having submitted yourself to a local board composed of your neighbors for the purpose of determining your availability for training and service in the land or naval forces of the United States, you are hereby notified that you have now been selected for training and service therein. Your friends and neighbors ask you to serve your country: You are to report for induction on August 4, 1943. ----------------------

Well, I hated to turn down my friends and neighbors, but I had just finished the first half of my senior year at Bedford High. Education had been a big issue in our family since the day I entered first grade at dear old Lincoln School in 1931. Neither of my parents had attended school beyond the eighth grade and they were determined that all three of their offspring would be High School graduates. My report card was examined carefully at the end of every grade period. The school was on the two semester system in those days. It nearly broke their hearts when I had pneumonia in the second grade and failed the first semester. They were happy again when I repeated and sailed through with a straight A card. However, no one suspected how that lost semester in 1932 would affect me in my senior class of 1943. I had finished the school year at Bedford High, one semester (six credits) short of the requirements needed to graduate. That failure in grade two had caught up with me and I did not graduate. I needed six hours to earn my diploma when I received my 'invitation' from Uncle Sam. I appealed to the three board members of the local Selective Service (draft board) for a deferment until I could complete the Fall semester and earn my High School diploma. They denied my request and the chairman said,

"I'm sorry Son, but we are taking everybody."

I replied,

"But you guys are still here!"

So that's how I got my free ride two weeks later when our little group of thirteen draftees boarded the Greyhound bus for Fort Benjamin Harrison in Indianapolis. I had experienced the hardships of life at home in the war for about eighteen months and now I would experience the war in uniform. Mom hung her blue star banner in the front window and High School started without me a week later.

I left an after school and Saturday job paying four bits (fifty cents) an hour. Uncle Sam took me out of school, gave a new suit, sent me to school, paid fifty dollars and promised an opportunity for rapid advancement. He kept his word and in a little over a year I got an ocean cruise and was a Tech Sergeant making $250 a month flying over Germany in a $250,000 plane! God and Mom's prayers brought me through twenty B-17 missions.

The war ended and I was 'Back home again in Indiana.' I went to Indiana University on the GI Bill and Uncle Sam paid my tuition and ninety dollars a month stipend. I graduated in three years and signed a teaching contract at Old Lincoln School for $300 a month.

We had won the war but the Depression was not over, but we rallied, met great challenges *and became the Greatest Generation.*

Addendum 2

Depression Boyhood of Robert F. Baugh

This addendum is to illustrate the severe boyhood experiences of a man who rose to become one of Bedford's most honored citizens. Bob Baugh served as Boys Club Director and a teacher for thirty- two years. He was a substitute father, counselor and advisor to thousands of boys because he recognized those needing help and understanding.

He served in the Army during WW Ii, fought on Iwo Jima and was awarded the Bronze Star. We came home from the war and met while going to college and I am proud to honor him as my best friend of fifty-six years.Bob contributed much to our community and lived by his favorite quote for boys:

"For each act there is an alternative,

Each person is the result of the choices he makes."

This story is from a brief autobiography.

Let the record show that I was born March 30, 1925 at St. Anthony's Hospital in Terre Haute, Indiana. I weighed only five pounds and my parents, Floyd Baugh and Anna Marie (Collier) Baugh, had even more worries when I developed measles and double pneumonia at age nine months. The Doctor told my parents I would probably live only three days but my Father was ill with tuberculosis and they decided to leave Terre Haute for Colorado because at that time many thought it had a better climate for TB patients. Two men accompanied my parents in an old Whippet automobile. It was an arduous trip in those days and an argument ensued between the two men and one threatened to kill the other. My father attempted to break up the dispute and a shotgun was fired, shooting one man's large toe off. He survived and lived into the 1990's. My mother later stated that the farther west we traveled toward Colorado, the better I became, so I survived the trip and in spite of the Terre Haute doctor's diagnosis.

On arriving in Cripple Creek, Colorado, my father and the two men established a whiskey still on Pikes Peak to make a living boot legging. This story was told to me by Tom Roelfson, Sheriff of Cripple Creek. (Rolefson, Cripple Creek pioneer of boom days in Cripple Creek) The Sheriff broke up their still after several complaints and got jobs for the men in the gold mines. My father, having lung problems, couldn't work in dust of the mines so the Sheriff gave him a job operating one of his ranches. The ranch was located about seventeen miles west from Cripple Creek. According to my mother, my Dad's TB seemed to be waning and he became physically stronger in the mountain air of Cripple Creek which had an elevation of about 9000 feet. He worked the Sheriff's ranch for five years, taking care of cattle and newborn calves.

I can barely recall a few things while living in Cripple Creek. I do remember the old winters and mild summers and that I managed to get into trouble a few times. Once I wandered away from the ranch house and fell asleep. The closest neighbor was about twelve miles from the ranch. The sheriff brought out some men to search for me. I was found about a mile away from the house sound asleep on a hillside. I also remember one time when I asked for an extra piece of pumpkin pie, but my eyes were bigger than my stomach and decided I didn't want it. Dad made me eat it anyway. On another occasion I was pushing a square wagon axle on two buggy wheels and rolling it down a slope. I ran into a fence post and smashed off the top of my left index finger. I was rushed into Cripple Creek to repair the injured finger and the doctor gave me a bag of gumdrops to get me to stop crying. My most memorable incident was the time my dad put on a Halloween mask and I was so scared that I ran into the outhouse and locked myself in. After crying for some time, I reluctantly returned to the house. I remember on several occasions when wildcats would get on the roof of the cabin at night and keep us awake, screaming. Dad would get his gun, but by the time he was outside, the wildcats were gone. One time Dad was hauling a wagon full of potatoes on a rough, steep road. The wagon overturned into a deep snow bank and my baby sister, Ruth, had to be dug out of the deep snow bank. No one was seriously hurt, but we lost lots of potatoes. Cars were a rare scene at the ranch but the sheriff had a Model T or Model A coupe and he would bring food and supplies out to the ranch house each week. Like most boys living on a ranch, I had a pony and a faithful dog, but I forget its name. We also had several horses and some pigs. One time little sister Ruth fell over the fence into the pig pen and had to be quickly gotten out. I remember that prairie dogs were a nuisance to the garden, particularly in potato patches. I also remember that I went deer hunting with my father one day in January 1930.

Tragedy struck our family a short time later when Dad went deer hunting one day when there was a heavy snow on the ground. He shot a large buck but didn't kill it – only wounded it. The snow was so deep that he went back to the house for his snowshoes and tracked the deer for several hours because and he didn't want it to suffer and we needed the meat

He finally gave up and returned to the ranch house but the next day he developed a bad case of pneumonia. My mother saddled a horse and rode seventeen miles to Cripple Creek to get a doctor. Dad was taken to the local hospital but died three days later on January 15th, 1930. I recall not being allowed to see him. I was not yet five years old and was kept out in the hallway. My father was buried at Mt. Pisgah Cemetery, High Park, Teller County, Colorado.

Suddenly, Mother was a widow with three small children and making preparations for our trip back to Indiana. A few days later I recall staying overnight in a hotel in Cripple Creek and I distinctly remember the very large headboard on that bed. The next morning we were on a train heading back to Terre Haute, Indiana, at the height of the Great Depression. Our little family was destitute and homeless. There were no jobs for men, let alone a widow with three children. There wasn't much government help at this time, which put millions on the streets without homes and food. Somehow we located in a small abandoned factory building. Several families, black and white, were living in this empty building. We had one large basement room with no water or electricity, a kerosene lamp and a small monkey stove (small two burner stove with an oven in the stove pipe). The building was located on First Street bounded on the west by the Wabash River and on the east by a railroad, which was bounded by a lane on each side. Nearby were the river bridge, a poultry house, creamery, and huge gas storage tank. The area was about three blocks from Main Street and the Courthouse Jail. This was to be my home for almost three years. (ages three to eight) Looking back on this period of time, it seems that it was much longer and more memorable. At age six, I was free to come and go wherever I wanted. Not much time was spent indoors, it was too hot in the summers and large rats were rampant in the building. I could hear them running over the floor at night.

Food was scarce and on a typical day we had a water gravy and corn cake breakfast, no lunch and boiled potatoes for dinner. Most kids were undernourished and suffered from illnesses connected with malnutrition. Periodically we would run alleys behind grocery stores to look for discarded spoiled vegetables and fruits or clipped bad parts (bananas, apples, oranges, potatoes, etc. I soon became involved with other boys in the area (many of whom later spent most of their lives in prison). We roamed around and did a lot of things that were dangerous and illegal. We sometimes searched for parked trucks with pop or fruit and often sneaked away with bottles of pop or a melon. We regularly traveled across town by 'hopping' rides on slow moving freight trains or street trolleys.

I would often visit Clyde's house on nearby Second Street and they would have a large pot of brown (pinto) beans with lots of watery soup. Occasionally Clyde's mother would allow me to eat with them and this was a treat that I have always remembered. I also remember a time of crime when I was the youngest of a gang of four boys age seven to nine. One evening, we entered a nearby house through the back kitchen door. We could hear people playing cards in an upstairs area. The older boys took some pop from an icebox (no refrigerator) and some jewelry from a bedroom. We left quietly and were never noticed but I was scared of being caught the whole time. Those boys weren't bad, just poor boys with little family support and a lot of free time on their hands.

Men were always thinking of ways to make money and in the summer, a group organized boxing bouts in a lighted area along the riverbank. Boys and men of all ages boxed each night and a small fee was charged to watch the fights. On occasion I would line up to box three rounds with another boy. I was eager to be asked to box because each of us received a bottle of pop and a hot dog after we fought. I was always hungry and looked forward to earning those treats.

Terre Haute had a lot of trains and they played an important role in people's lives by providing a way to ride from one end of town to the other. We kids hopped trains often for free rides across town. On one occasion, I got caught on top of a boxcar moving through town. It was picking up speed on its way to Chicago. Someone spotted me and got the train stopped. They called my mother to come and get me and she pounded on me all the way back home. In fall and winter we would hop a train in the south end of town, climb the coal cars and stack coal on the ledge of the car so we could push it off near our home. People would be waiting with carts to haul the coal away to provide fuel for the cold winter days. Police were called but never made a serious effort to catch anyone because they knew winter was particularly harsh on poor people.

I know that in those troubled times I caused mother much grief. Food and fuel were difficult to come and we looked forward to the Government's milk program issued by the Salvation Army. We had to take our own bucket and I recall standing in long lines on cold mornings with my mother, eager to get a free gallon of milk. This was a very special treat because if you wanted gravy for breakfast or something to drink other than water you had to steal it from trucks or vendors on the streets.

I can't remember exactly how long we lived in Terre Haute. I know that we arrived from Cripple Creek in January 1930, two months before my fifth birthday and left when I was almost eight. I remember starting the first grade at age seven at Crawford's School about three blocks away on Third Street. I don't remember much about my school experience except that most of my classmates were poor or destitute, hungry and often malnourished. Many kids fell asleep in class including me. I slept so much in class that the school authorities referred me to the local health officer. I was examined and it was determined that my infected tonsils needed to come out. This procedure was done in a doctor's office and it took two nurses and my mother to hold me down to administer the ether. I remember the doctor asking me to name things I liked to eat. I got as far as oranges and suddenly the lights went out. Ether is a terrifying experience for a small child. I was taken back to our little rat infested basement room after the surgery.

One day we were playing a circle game at school when I spotted a string on the floor and I told the teacher there was something on the floor and that temporarily broke the students' attention. The teacher slapped my face and told me to get back in line and pay attention to what was going on. Needless to say, I never volunteered info again. I remembered her name for years and forgot it till now, however she shall remain unknown because I'll not volunteer that info. Poor as we were, a government health program provided cod liver oil for all students and a spoonful of the awful tasting stuff was dispensed from a bottle. School officials recognized city-wide health problems among children and one day we all received smallpox vaccinations the result of those vaccinations were big scabs which produced large lifetime scars on each student's shoulder. The happiest day at school was the instituting of free lunches, which consisted of hot vegetable soup and crackers. The school lunch program was one of the most effective local programs for near starving children. My school attendance improved because I went to school every day to get that free lunch.

We finally moved from the basement of the vacant factory building to an old frame house farther south on First Street. My mother's family relatives lived in one half of the house and we now had two rooms but still no water or electricity. Some of the names were Aunt Emma (bent over from an uncorrected broken back), her husband Frank and sons, Orville, Floyd, and Bob. She bore all her children with this handicap, a result of climbing a fence and falling, breaking her back. Other relatives lived nearby and Uncle Jim's family had two daughters. He was a bootlegger who peddled products from various neighborhood stills. There were several houses of prostitution in the neighborhood and twenty-five cents was the going fee for this service. The Depression forced people to commit crimes and 'anyway, to earn a little money' was the rule: bootlegging, prostitution, stealing or begging for handouts were ways to survive.

This house faced the railroad, as the other location did and one near fatal day my four-year old sister, Ruth, ran into the street following another child. She got into the street and saw a car coming, panicked, turned and ran back toward the house directly into the path of a car. Her body was tossed into the air and she landed on her back on the railroad track. She suffered severe head and back injuries and remained in critical condition for a week. After recovery, she had a scar from her forehead to the center of her scalp, her kidneys were damaged and were a problem for the remainder of her life. Christmas at our home was not much celebrated and we never had a tree or special treats. However, we would go to the Light House Mission, (which existed for many years) and each child received a small toy, a sack of candy, and an orange. I still vividly remember receiving that sack of hard candy. These were thrills that were never forgotten.

I discovered the Terre Haute Boys' Club at about the age of seven and thought it was a great place. However, on one of my visits, I entered the gym where a few boys were shooting baskets. The ball bounded toward me and one of the boys called for the ball but I threw it to the other end of the gym. You probably have guessed what happened next. That kid beat the tar out of me and I didn't go near the gym much after that experience. I did, however, visit the club several times. The Club director was Ted Moore, and the building was an old structure located near where the newer building stands today. (Ted was still the director for a time during my directorship at Bedford.)

Across the river was a neighborhood called Taylorville which some referred to as Tin Town. It was located just off the riverbank and sometimes flooding would drive the people from their homes, most of which were wood and tin shacks, some had dirt floors. Farmers had better shelters for their animals than most of the people living in Taylorville. These people were the poorest of the poor and many were involved in crimes of robbery, boot-legging and even murder but Terre Haute police seldom crossed the river to investigate. I recall that for some reason I was sent to Taylorville to live with my Great Aunt for awhile. It was probably because Mom needed help. I only knew her as Aunt Onie, she was overweight, a chain smoker, and not very healthy but she was good to me and the meals were better than at home. Mom's Uncle Louis died in prison from injuries incurred by a falling barrel. Orville was paroled and managed to buy an old truck to make money hauling away ashes from homes. I attended a one room school in Taylorville for a brief time and I remember that he took me to Terre Haute and bought me new pants, a shirt and shoes. I was really proud of those new clothes because they were the first I ever had. Orville was basically a good person but drank a lot to escape his personal problems. He had married but had no children and was later divorced. He passed away shortly after Betty and I were married. We attended the funeral in Terre Haute, a pauper's funeral, at the Light House Mission across the street from the Court House. I was sorry that Orville, one of the few persons who were good to me during my impoverished boyhood, died a destitute and lonely man at a very young age.

I remember being glad to leave Taylorsville to return to my home in Terre Haute. Aunt Onie had married a cook on one of the trains. I remember his name as being Charlie and everyone referred to him as Uncle Charlie. I don't remember his last name but he was a nice man and he often brought candy. He cut his thumb cutting meat on the train and infection set in. The doctor removed his thumb, later his hand and then his arm. He died shortly after the arm was removed. I recall attending the funeral in a small place on Second or Third Street. Aunt Onie died shortly after we moved to Bedford

Each year an organization conducted an Easter Egg hunt at Deming Park on the east side of Terre Haute. I went with other boys in the neighborhood to take part in the hunt and didn't find many eggs, but I did find one that was painted red, white, and blue. It was a special prize egg and I received a certificate for five dollars which was to be used at a local clothing store. I bought a complete outfit of clothing: shirt, pants, and shoes. Five dollars was a lot of money in 1932 and I remember that moment as if it happened yesterday!

Summing up other memories in Terre Haute, I recall cleaning milk cans at a nearby creamery. My pay was a gallon bucket of ice cream, which was a real treat for the family. Also close by was a poultry house and occasionally a chicken would get loose during the unloading. We would catch the chicken and sell it for a dime. One day another boy and I took keys from a loaded ice truck and buried them in the sand on the riverbank. A neighbor lady saw us take the keys and told my mother. I knew if we didn't go find the keys I would get the broomstick around the back of my legs. Somehow we found the keys we had buried in the sand, but I got the broomstick anyway!

As I previously stated, most children in the area were largely unsupervised and often engaged in risky activities. The Wabash river was an area where many of us spent a lot of time. I could swim a little and I recall diving near the riverbank and discovering what appeared to be a stolen bicycle, which had been tossed of the bridge. As a dare challenge, I remember crawling across the Wabash River Bridge on the beam located under it. I was probably about six years old at the time.

A turning point in the lives of our family occurred when one day a man and woman drove up to our house in a new car. I was told it was my Uncle Clarence and his wife Ruth. They came to inform us that we had inherited a portion of another uncle's insurance policy. His name was Uncle Roy, he was a WWI vet who had been gassed, which contributed to his early death. The amount inherited was $2000, a lot of money in those days. We soon gathered a few items of clothing and took a train to Bedford. Our only tie to Lawrence County was the fact that my Dad, Floyd Baugh was born May 28, 1901 in Avoca, Indiana and had relatives here.

In a way it was sad leaving the area and the friends that I played with daily. To this day I can recall the First Street area, the river and the friends I left behind. At the time, as a seven-year-old, I didn't want to leave Terre Haute. Even with extreme poverty and little hope for any future, it was all I had ever known. I always wondered about those friends and how their miserable lives turned out. Looking back now, I can say that the boys I left behind never had a chance in life. They were destined to spend most of their lives in prison and experience an early death. Years later I got information about some of those boys of First Street from Ted Moore, the Boys' Club director.

Leaving Terre Haute in 1933 changed the direction of my life for the better. My family, friends and life achievements, such as the may have been, would not have taken place had we stayed in Terre Haute. The cruel environment would no doubt have had a negative impact on our family's future. Arriving in Bedford (Lawrence County) was like entering into a new world.

We lived with Uncle Clarence Baugh and his family at Leesville for a few weeks until we could find a home to buy. I enrolled in the one room schoolhouse in Leesville. The room was divided by a sheet or curtain to make two rooms, but I was there for only a brief time. We checked out houses in different areas of the county and almost bought one near Heltonville. We finally decided on a house located in Breckenridge, an area near the north edge of Bedford. The cost of the house with an acre of ground was $500. It was a three room tar paper shack, with no electricity or plumbing. Not many homes at this time had indoor plumbing, most had a drilled a well with a pump. That house is where I spent my formative years and started taking school more seriously; which meant that I attended most every day.

Moving to Lawrence County didn't take us out of poverty. The inherited money was divided between three kids and my mother. The kids' money was placed in a trust fund where we were allowed to draw out a total of $3.00 a month. That source of income soon ran out. My mother had not yet married and we relied on food orders issued by the Township Trustee to get by. Mother was a good cook, she worked hard to feed her family and with federal government surplus help we received food rations of flour, lard, butter and some canned meats. Living in a tar paper shack in the summer was hot and we spent much time outside. Flies, mosquitoes, and chiggers kept most people in a miserable state and on hot nights we would take a blanket and sleep outside. However, the winters were very cold in that tar paper shack. Sometimes it was so cold in the house that water in the water bucket would freeze. Most people reading this probably don't know what the water bucket was for. It was kept filled and to use for drinking and washing little hands and faces.

The Dive School Principal started me in the second grade but soon moved me to the third. Ruby Hall was the first and secnd grade teacher and she later married the Principal, Harold Brinegar. Being a new kid in the community, every boy my age or older wanted to fight. I got beaten up several times until I learned the game. The theory was to never back down and to be sure if you had to fight that you struck the first hard blow to the face. This was often enough to end the fight. After every kid had his turn with me, I was accepted into the group.

So I entered Dive School in the 3rd grade as a nine year old and the school was relatively new. The main upper story had four large rooms, each having two grade levels, one through eight and only four teachers including the principal who also taught two grades. My attitude toward school wasn't enthusiastic. I worked just hard enough to pass. The school year started after Labor Day and usually concluded by April 21st or 22nd. The short school year allowed the boys to be free to help with spring planting of crops. I don't recall having much homework or taking books home, but I usually made C's and B's and always placed high in each class on the Standard Benet National tests used to determine student IQs. Teachers I remember well were the Principal, Harold Brinegar, who later got his doctorate and taught at IU for many years. Another teacher was fifth and sixth grade teacher, Robert Ferguson, who was later killed in WWII. There were two other teachers I didn't have but remember well. One year in the sixth grade I had Opal Ford who later succeeded Brinegar as Principal. In the eighth grade, I was considered the one student most likely **not** to succeed. Actually I was the only one of my class to graduate with a college degree --- so much for predictions.

Some of my memorable moments as a student at Dive was playing on the basketball team. Principal, Harold Brinegar, transported the team to area schools in his car, probably without pay. Some of the Jr. High teams we played were Springville, Needmore, Heltonville, Shawswick, Trinity Springs, and Oolitic. There were other teams, but I can't remember them. One very popular activity of the time was shooting marbles and I left several boys crying and angry as I often won most of their favorite marbles in games played after school. I stored hundreds of marbles in old tobacco sacks and claimed them as spoils of victory. Occasionally I lost some of my best marbles on bad days. Some of the boys were very good and would win local contests. When I was an eighth grader, I won the Dive School Tournament which entitled me to participate in the County Marble Tourney held at Thornton Park. After several rounds, darkness set in with only two players remaining – myself and a boy from Shawswick by the name of Kern, I have forgotten his first name but I see him around occasionally. The tourney director, Russ Baker, declared the tourney a tie and declared the both of us County Champs. There was one wooden trophy (turned on a lathe and finished with varnish). A coin was flipped to see who would receive the trophy and Kern won the toss and the trophy. Somewhere in my scrambled collections is a news article about the tourney. This favorite pastime gave way to other activities as families acquired more income. Temporarily the student most likely not to succeed was a popular hero for a day or two at the school. It is a shame that they say fame is fleeting, because that was one of my proudest moments.

It seemed that the time I spent living in Breckenridge was a very long time, but actually it was only about ten years. A lot of things took place in this time period: achievements, disappointments, and hopes – always hopes. We didn't have great expectations, just little things which would make life better.

I don't exactly remember, but a few years after leaving Terre Haute my mother Anna, married her second cousin, Curtis Melvin Elkins. He was several years younger than my mother, but he was a hard worker and got his first job hauling coal for the Cosner Coal Company. Soon the family would enlarge and Anna and Curtis' first child was a boy followed in regular order by three girls. Ours was one of the largest and poorest families in the Dive School or Breckenridge community. The house was so crowded that I spent a great amount of time away. This time spent fending for myself taught me several life experience lessons that pretty much shaped my personality and thinking that remain with me today.

This is not to imply that my mother wasn't a powerful influence on my life. Her example of daily hard work to feed and clothe seven children under extremely trying conditions was inspiring. She did all this work without any of the things we take for granted today. For instance imagine you are responsible for the welfare of nine individuals without indoor plumbing, (no bathroom) kitchen appliances such as refrigerators, electric gas or stove or dishwasher. There was no washing machine, so all clothing was scrubbed by hand on a washboard, rung out by hand and hung to dry. Providing three meals daily for such a large number consumed most of her time and energy. Her life was a living hell and if there is a heaven, she surely has a place reserved. At the age of forty-five, she looked eighty. In her later years after all of the children were gone from home, even in failing health, she enjoyed a few years of peace and rest from her life-long grind to raise a large family during the most difficult period in our history.

I'm talking about the Great Depression which lasted throughout the 1930s and into the early '40s. My mother was religious but did not attend any church. She was always kind and considerate of everyone and I never knew her to lie, cheat or even set a bad example for her children. Her only vice was smoking and I suppose she started smoking before I was born and continued up into her late forties. Smoking was the little pleasure she had each day but breathing problems and other conditions forced her to give up her cigarettes.

Again I say, that because of the large family living under harsh circumstances, my mother paid little attention to what I was doing. The only requirements for each day was that I had to pump all the water she needed for the day, fill up the coal bins and to cut enough kindling to start the fire the next morning. I was free to be on my own after my chores were done. My Breckenridge days were filled with activities that today' youth would see childish or uninteresting. The years seemed long and the days were filled with simple pleasures. Since all of the area families were affected by the economic depression, most had to depend upon the government to provide food and the bare essentials for clothing and other needs. A family earning twenty-five dollars a week was considered middle Income. The family car was usually an old model and in the early thirties, few teens were allowed to drive or own an auto. Federal programs created by President Roosevelt's National Recovery Act (NRA), the New Deal provided food, clothing and jobs for the very poor. Periodically, we would pick up commodities: food staples (flour, sugar, canned meat, cheese, hominy flakes, etc.) Work programs called WPA and PWA began and paid $12.00 a week. I recall joining an Oolitic High School student work program called the National Youth Administration (NYA). I was paid four dollars a month to work after school dusting erasers, washing blackboards, and emptying wastebaskets. Later, a program called the Civilian Conservation Corps (CCC), was put in place to recruit men eighteen and over to live in work camps performing conservation activities. I was about to sign up for the CCC program working out of Spring Mill Park when I received my draft papers. Later most CCC recruits were drafted into the armed services. Meanwhile I was an Army private drawing fifty bucks a month!

A lot of things took place in the poverty of my childhood: achievements, disappointments, and hopes — always hopes. We didn't have great expectations, just little things to make life better. Robert F. Baugh

About the Author

James Lee Hutchinson's fifth book of short stories is an Indiana Bicentennial project telling of boys in Southern Indiana during the Great Depression of 1930 -1942 and a 'pre-quel' to his Eighth Air Corps books. The hardships of children who lacked food and lived in homes with no plumbing, electricity or central heat are unknown to this generation. They 'skinny dipped' in the creek or roamed fields and woods. Their lives were not complicated by bathrooms, air conditioning, television, computer games or cell-phones. Youngsters of the pre-war Depression survived poverty, fought as teenagers in World War II and came home to make the United States a world power. They were the Greatest Generation.

The author holds three Indiana University degrees and is retired from 37 years as elementary teacher, Principal and Assistant to Superintendent. He is a fifty year Mason, Rotary Paul Harris Fellow and Presbyterian Elder.

The 91 year old Eighth Air Corps veteran flew 20 missions as a B-17 Radio Operator/gunner as a teenager. He speaks and writes to report WW II history from an old man who was there as a teenager. He has preserved 200 short stories of World War ll veterans.

Through These Eyes -- Bombs Away -- Boys in the B-17 --- B-17 Memories

INSERT BOOKS

I shall be telling this with a sigh Somewhere ages and ages hence:
Two roads diverged in a wood, and I— I took the one less traveled by,
And that has made all the difference.

Robert Frost

CPSIA information can be obtained
at www.ICGtesting.com
Printed in the USA
BVHW032241130719
553143BV00018B/1/P